Everything starts at the mome

This book is not about fortune telling. It's simply a way to connect you with time in a way that has you aligned with who you are at your essence.

The time of your birth was a unique moment in the development of the universe. That moment in time was as unique for you as your DNA or your fingerprints. You are of that moment. Everything about you springs from that. You are the vintage wine that could only have been created there and then. Your time fingerprint, your Time DNA...when you were born, has a huge impact on your future.

When your birthdate interfaces with the 9 Star Ki Calendar it plants a new seed. Within this seed lies the gift of understanding and tapping into your Contextual Winning Field. Use this book to understand it, and unlock your true potential. Prepare to be amazed!

What people are saying about Rex

"The experience of being in the hands of Rex Lassalle brings wisdom to the deepest healing. The depth and breadth of his knowledge seems to know no bounds and his highly developed senses of listening tunes into the exact area of tension needing release.

The work I received from Rex brought me insights that I will be exploring for years to come. My body and my deepening understanding of how to care for myself is a lifelong process and I now feel I have been given the correct tools and insights into how to live in tune with my unique rhythm.

The experience of receiving his work is second to none. I only wish everyone I know and love could be as privileged as I have been to work with him. I cannot thank Rex enough for his healing presence and endlessly insightful wisdom."

Gillian Duffin - Structural Integration Practitioner, Dublin, Ireland

Rex combines a wealth of insights from his work as a Shiatsu practitioner with his deep understanding of the Oriental Five Element Theory and Nine Star Ki Astrology into a unique system of understanding "that time has another dimension beyond linear measurement".

Time carries discernible qualities which have an ongoing influence on us. Rex refers to this system as "Grasshopping," and has helped many of his clients to discover skilful ways of handling life's challenges, resolving emotional disturbances and, on a deeper level, understanding why they are driven to do what they do. His first book "Grasshopping Through Time' was published in 1999. Rex's continuous commitment to Zen practice and the understanding and insight gained through such practice infuse his classes and private sessions with a deep listening to what is really present.

Your Contextual Winning Field is really your Time Matrix, and is related to the day on which you were born. From the Oriental perspective of Five Element theory, there are certain patterns based upon the qualities which these elements manifest. The elements in question are referred to as Fire, Earth, Metal, Water and Wood, and there's a whole dance that goes on between them which creates the entire context of your life: and connecting with an understanding of how these elements interact can make a huge difference as regards living your life, dealing with your stress levels and handling your relationships.

A Story

Some years ago, one of my clients was a lady who had major challenges with her relationship with her children, along with some big challenges in her personal life. Her contextual winning field pattern was the five earth star, and with that pattern, the supportive colour is yellow. In chatting with her, I started to ask some questions.

I said: "By the way, your kitchen, what colour is it painted?"

She replied, "Well, my kitchen is painted green."

And I said, "So do you have problems in your kitchen?"

She says, "Yes, I have major problems, nearly all the devices that I have in my kitchen keep breaking down. I recently got a washing machine, it broke down, I have problems with my stove and in fact a lot of arguments with my kids happen when we're in the kitchen."

I then asked, "This son of yours who is causing a lot of problems: tell me his birthday."

It turned out that his contextual winning field pattern was eight, the supportive colour of which is a similar kind of yellow to the number 5 CWF (perhaps moving a little more towards orange)

I said, "Well, I have a suggestion to make for you. You need to paint your kitchen yellow."

She said, "Really?"

I said, "Well try it: I mean, is it working how it is right now?"

She said, "No it isn't."

So I asked her: "So what do you have to lose, except maybe the cost of the paint and the time to do the painting?

So anyway she did it. She called me back two weeks later, and said: "Rex, I can't believe this. My son who had been giving me a hard time, he came into the kitchen a few days after it had been painted, put his hands around my waist, said 'I love you' and then, 'Mum, I want to help you with the kitchen, with washing up the dishes'. And he's a whole different person and a lot of the problems I'd had with kitchen have somehow cleared up, strange as this may sound, my washing machine works fine now, different things like that."

Personally, this freaked me out. I hadn't expected all of these things to happen, and so quickly. And since that time, I've seen similar things occurring for many people in different situations, not only with the colours that they use or wear, but other things that have gone on for them.

I can only tell you what I have observed.

Life is really simple,
but we insist on
making it complicated.

Confucius

REX LASSALLE

Rex Lassalle is a world-renowned Master in the Japanese healing art of Shiatsu and an authority on Oriental Astrology and it's impact on health. He is also an experienced osteopath and Aikidoka (practitioner of Aikido).

During the past four decades, Rex has been right at the cutting edge of bodywork practices in Europe and further afield. He helped to establish the East West Centre and Community Health Foundation in London in 1976, and set up his own Hara Shiatsu School in London in 1986. By the mid 1980s, Rex had amassed a wealth of insights from his work, which he combined with his deep understanding of Oriental five element theory and Nine Star Ki Astrology to develop a unique system of understanding that Time itself has another dimension beyond simple linear measurement. Rex observed that Time carries very specific discernible qualities, and that these qualities are discernible and have an ongoing influence upon us.

At the core of all that I am sharing and explaining in this book, is the idea of MAKING TIME YOUR FRIEND.

This is what the Contextual Winning Field is all about. With our modern education, we were never been given this perception of Time. Time was always something that was gobbling us up like some monster, and what is profoundly sad is that we have not explored time from any other perspective than 24/7, end of story.

I would say that this is true for 99.999% of us. And yet Time is something that has given us an entry point into life. She is the one who, when we arrived on planet earth as a baby, gave us our "Time Matrix".

Yes, astrologers may have looked at it from the perspective of which planets were moving where in the sky, and what was happening with the Moon etc. but very, very few of us have gone up to Time and said, "THANK YOU for bringing me here on to the planet at this Time. You gave me that moment, TIME. Please tell me how to be friendly with you and with that moment of TIME when you brought me here. Please show me."

Yes, I know you have other currents pulling on you and creating other waves but at the foundation, at the core, there is YOU.

Dear readers, this is what I am truly asking you to explore. The tools and skills that I have shared here are not the be-all and end-all of making TIME your friend. It is an introduction, it is an acknowledgement, inviting TIME to show you more of her support and wisdom as you remain receptive to her influence and presence in your life.

Your Contextual Winning Field tool is an introduction to getting to know her in your life as a friend and a moment-by moment-companion, as she is always there wherever you are. She is inherent in your shadow, your blood and your DNA. Isn't it time that you truly connect with her in a friendly and relaxed way?

The book you are holding in your hands will help you to do just that. Your Contextual Winning Field will allow you to experience a new source of freedom and self-expression. With the guidance of your Contextual Winning Field, you'll discover and experience this new freedom and self-expression, and you'll be able to say to yourself, "Now, Time really IS my friend!"   Enjoy the friendship.

Time is the coin of your life.
It is the only coin you have,
and only you can determine
how it will be spent.
Be careful lest you
let other people
spend it for you.

Carl Sandburg

We are born at a given moment,
in a given place and,
like vintage years of wine,
we have the qualities of the year
and of the season
of which we are born.
Astrology does not
lay claim to anything more.

Carl Jung

THE TIME OF YOUR LIFE

Could it be now?

Rex Lassalle

Published by
Filament Publishing Ltd
16, Croydon Road, Waddon, Croydon,
Surrey, CR0 4PA, United Kingdom
Telephone +44 (0)20 8688 2598
Fax +44 (0)20 7183 7186
info@filamentpublishing.com
www.filamentpublishing.com

ISBN 978-1-908691-91-0

Printed by Berforts Information Press
Stevenage & Hastings

Dedication

Dedicated to Francesco D'Amore, for introducing me to the world of alchemy, with profoundly simple explanations of what it is all about, and most importantly for giving me a model that I could use to confirm my views about the Contextual Winning Field and its correlation to specific colours.

In my research into the 9 Star Ki Astrology system, Francesco's willingness to teach me with great humour and salty, down-to-earth examples allowed me to look with new eyes at ways of viewing and working with this material. Sincere gratitude to you, Francesco: you gave me a way of knowing and assessing things that changed my life.

This book is also dedicated to Monica Zanchi for her tireless efforts in translating my endless questions to Francesco, and also for spending hours driving me back and forth for discussions about alchemy with Francesco. You made it possible for me to access this new way seeing.

Acknowledgements

To my parents Max and Veronica Lassalle, for their ever-present guidance, communication and presence in my life as this work unfolded. They were always there to open doors to new insights and applications of the Contextual Winning Field, in their own unique way of giving me feedback.

To John Lewis, for his continuing enthusiasm for my work on the Contextual Winning Field: he has always been there over the last decade, editing my efforts and spending hour upon hour bringing in fresh information to the project, and most importantly in engaging me with challenging conversations about the relevance of my research, along with what I had written, and how I had written it. Without John's efforts, this book would not have been published.

To Gioacchino Allasia, for organizing that very special Contextual Winning Field seminar in December 2003 where a lot of the ideas and views in this book were first taught. His trust and support for my work has contributed to me pushing the boundaries of how I present this material, and the context in which I do so.

To Margherita Dressadore, for being there at that special Wisdom Star seminar in 2003 in Florence and for introducing me to Francesco. This was a blessing of Destiny showing its hand.

To Marc Salmon, for his support in providing accommodation through challenging times when I was in transition. I also want to thank him for his enthusiastic willingness to run diagnostic tests using alchemic remedies and their correspondence to Contextual Winning Field colours from the model that evolved through my talks with Francesco the alchemist. The 100% confirmation that these remedies showed, based on their colour emanations, gave my observations a reality with global relevance.

To Dr Anthony Soyer, for his total willingness in offering me an on-going generous listening to my ideas and observations, yet at the same time asking succinct questions. This always took my work deeper, blowing away the chaff from the seed.

To Bettina Duesmann for organising the numberless files on my computer. This allowed me to collate this book in a way that stimulated new angles for me to present my work. Thanks for also pointing out that at times what I was writing was self-talk and that the general public would have no idea what I was writing about. Thanks for your support in having this book ripen.

To Hartmut Hauser, for offering me unexpected feedback about the relevance of my work in social and political circles. His feedback confirmed ideas I had about the responses of certain Contextual Winning Field patterns in stressful circumstances.

To Andre Poppe, for continually inviting me to present my work to audiences in Belgium, who at times knew nothing about this way of looking at life. He always encouraged me to share how the subtle influence of many everyday responses can support us in realising certain goals, or sabotaging them if inappropriate. On another note, I need to acknowledge that Andre is the most innovative shiatsu practitioner that I have ever met in my 4 decades of working in this field. I always learn some effective new approaches from interacting with him. Thanks, Andre.

To Ruth Van Buren, for giving me in-depth feedback about my observations, coming from her experience with family, close friends and business associates. These pearls of wisdom added a clarity and precision to many of my observations.

To Johan Taft, for his friendship and practical advice regarding ways of making my work relevant to business executives, coming from his work as a business coach and mentor.

To Yvonne Smith, for inviting me to work at the Mandarin Oriental Spa in London: this opportunity allowed me to spend many years distilling my work on The Contextual Winning Field, as it enabled me to take care of basic living needs.

To Winnie Hewitt, for her core interest in my work and for often sending me information about personalities and specific characteristics that she observed: this always gave me fresh ways of seeing things.

To Viram Wijnhoven, for his feedback about my work in a blunt and direct manner that was always humorous and at times totally outrageous, yet always relevant.

To Annie Terry, for her open sharing of her work with sound and psychotherapy. In our conversations she always brought a new way for me to listen to what was occurring with my clients and patients, which inadvertently had a knock-on effect in my discerning new distinctions about the Contextual Winning Field patterns. Your sharing brought a new richness to my work.

To Tuula Styrman, for organizing a number of programs in Helsinki, Finland about the Contextual Winning Field which were always a great success, with a lot of sharing from participants.

To Greg Lassalle, for continually introducing me to new singers and musicians through YouTube, which consistently inspired my creative process and which had the effect of pushing the boundaries of my work. Chatting with Greg has a way of opening my senses to a more spacious and fresh way of experiencing things and from this, new insights occurred.

To Gary Young and his Young Living Essential Oils, the consumption of which during the past 2 years has sharpened my intuition and brought a youthful vitality and vibrancy along with a capacity to have sharper, more focused concentration. I have also discovered that certain Young Living Essential Oils are a great source of support in being connected with your Contextual Winning Field.

To Lena Gelin for her friendship and deep sharing of her perceptions of life and the dynamics she observed in her family and in other families from her work with them. Her sharing of these dynamics had visual qualities to it, which she would describe in a precise manner. She would often share birthdates with me, as she knew that I had a deep curiosity for the time DNA of the person she was describing.

This then stacked up many gems of information that at times would reveal themselves to me as I wrote this book. Thanks, Lena.

To Jukka-Pekka Lilja, for his ongoing search for humour in any life situation, yet within the laughter he would make a very sharp distinction that would just register as being true and very real. A smiling Taoist Finn with a subtle gentle energy that he imparts with all that he does. Thanks for the teaching you bring to me every time we meet.

To Boogsie Sharpe, for his musical arrangements for steel band, and also for his incredible playing of the instrument with a spontaneity that always left me sensing that he was simply in the moment with his creativity. This inspired me to adopt the same approach as I worked on this book. Something that I have heard at times from Trinidadians in the last 5 years after watching Boogsie's arrangement of Michael Jackson's "Billie Jean" by his Phase II orchestra on YouTube: they have often said, "If Michael had met Boogsie and heard what he did, Quincy Jones would never have been his arranger." Thank you Boogsie, for your awesome creativity.

To Red Garland, whose piano playing had a touch and feeling and nuance that I had never heard before. This opened my mind to the possibility that the same creative sensitivity was available to me as I wrestled with my observations about The Contextual Winning Field.

To Bezawork Asfaw and her singing of "BUNA": this was a song that I listened to many, many times when things were stuck with what I was doing with this book. I had no idea what she is singing about, as I know nothing about the Ethiopian language. Her staying in the same chord throughout the song was a hint for me to stay focused, as there are other ways of doing what I am doing though looking at the "same window." Thank you, Bezawork.

To Haimanot Girma and her song "GOT TO SEE". Again, this is an Ethiopian song, and I have no idea what is being said, yet the hint "Got To See" and her voice and the arrangement of her music allowed me to see new things with what I was doing. Thanks, Haimanot.

To Carlos Santana, and the timelessness of his music and arrangements. A link that has been there continually over the last four decades that facilitates a continuity of thought and experiences from Trinidad where I first heard his music in the late 60s to the present moment. His sound just keeps getting better and better, and allows the opening of new creative portals within me as I hear what he does with his music. Thanks, Carlos.

To Chris Day, for his smooth confidence in pulling this book together and truly grasping what this book is about and his skillful way of presenting my work with grace and elegance. Your sense of humour, compassionate attitude and patience has been a joyful presence to have as I completed this book.

To Helena Holrick, for her tireless efforts in showing me other ways to presenting what I am doing in a way that would be relevant to the reader, and for encouraging me to think about it in that way as I completed the book.

To Yvette Taylor and her team, for distilling the things that were needed to present this material in the digital world that talks to people with where they are. Thank you, Yvette, for your concerted and diligent efforts on my behalf.

To Dwayne Essex and Adolphus Lutango, for their enthusiastic input on many levels, especially with respect to retail outlet logistics and core business strategies.

Finally, I would like to acknowledge the thousands of students who have attended my classes over many decades. These classes were always my research laboratory, where I was able to discover patterns that were present for these students in terms of their health, relationships, money, career and travel. Thanks for all your open, deep sharing.

Emma Petrov is a Finnish artist who captures the core essences of people with her drawings. She was born and raised in rural Finland, and was given private painting lessons from professional artist Marika Holm when she was 15. Later on, she attended the Porvoo School for Industrial Arts and Crafts from 2007 to 2009. Since that time, she has taken part in several art exhibitions in Tammisaari, Finland, and done work for a number of magazines. Emma created the sketches of the 18

Contextual Winning Field unconscious masters and the sketch of Marina Abramovic for this book. She painstakingly got "in the zone" to capture the magnificence of these global icons.

I am very aware that what Emma puts on the paper is not a "doing". Her work is an entering into the Spirit of the individual, and then inviting them onto the page. Thank you, Emma, for the magnificent artistic distillations that you have brought to life here: I feel deeply honoured to have your creations in my book.

Footnote

It may come as a surprise to many of you reading this page how much acknowledgement I have given to music and songs by people who I have never met. This is no mystery, as my childhood was one of growing up in a soundscape and somehow I am always seeking to link those childhood imprints to things around me in the moment, and this nourishes me.

When that childhood aspect of yourself feels nourished and supported, creativity flows much more smoothly. A child at play is then present. No mystery at all, just life and its many blessings being celebrated.

Do not dwell in the past,
do not dream of the future,
concentrate the mind
on the present moment.

Buddha

Table of Contents

THE TIME OF YOUR LIFE

There was a gentleman by the name of Bertie Marshall who is known in Trinidad as the Master Innovator of the steel pan - or the steel drum as we refer to it in the UK. It was his research and his work that took it to where it is today.

INTRODUCTION
The Story begins

Many years ago when I came across the 9 Star Ki system I was initially very sceptical about it. I thought it maybe had a relevance in ancient Japan, Asia or China but I didn't necessarily think that this system was relevant for modern life in the West. However, my curiosity was aroused.

I have always been drawn towards patterns that I would observe around me, largely due to the influence of my parents as I grew up in Trinidad.

The period in which I grew up was one where the society was coming alive with new creations. The steel band movement had been around for a while but it hadn't really broken through into the area of total social acceptance within Trinidad society.

There was this edge there as regards creating things, pushing them to the limits. I found this was present with musicians, singers and the people around them. The education system was very intense, too in the sense that you had to listen to teachers, unlike the present day! Teachers and parents ruled the roost. What they said, you had to do. There was no compromise. This regime sharpened my mind, and it had a big influence on me as to how I engaged with life. Passion was a key ingredient that arose from this.

My parents most certainly triggered a major interest in looking beyond everyday life. An obvious example was the fact that everyone was saying that seven was a lucky number and yet my mother would say, "Rex, 13 is a lucky number". She would make most of her purchases for the month on the 13th of the month and if it was Friday the 13th, she would be buying a lot of different lottery tickets or taking chances in gambling, and she often won.

On my father's side, he had a whole attitude of questioning life. When I would repeat to my father something I had read, he would ask "Rex, you really believe that?" and then he would indicate to me certain situations where this could not be true. So this encouraged me to always seek out my own truth, and I became sensitive to seeing meaning in the things around me.

For example, if a grasshopper landed on the table in front of us, my mother or my father would say, well so-and-so is going to happen. And I would ask them, "How can you say that? Why would you say that?" And they would answer, "Child, listen, don't ask stupid questions, just watch, you will see." And I would observe what they had said, and invariably it was the case.

What they pointed out arose from the patterns that they observed around them. After a while, I stopped questioning what they said and started observing and learning instead. When I went to college, there was this incredible teacher of mathematics called Father Lai Fook who was a magician with numbers. Professors from the University of the West Indies used to come to him for advice because of the great clarity he had with numbers. I was very fortunate to have bee taught by him.

So when I began looking at numbers in the 9 Star Ki system, it was very comfortable for me as numbers were for me another type of music, to look at and play with.

I started to get this capacity to observe patterns without having to validate them: The 9 Star Ki system allowed me freedom of thought and freedom of mind in looking at the patterns that I observed around me, which helped me to draw certain distinctions from sequences that I consistently saw happening.

One of the aspects of this was my observations relating to people's birth dates. Later on, when working as a shiatsu practitioner, one of the questions I would naturally ask my clients was their date of birth, and also seek to find out as much as I could about their health history.

Based on that, I started to develop a way of looking at their pattern, trying to spot the high stress periods in their life. My clients were surprised at how accurate my descriptions of their lives were, just based on this simple information.

At the time, I couldn't explain how I was doing this, and I didn't even have a name for it. This was just the start. It was within the 9 Star KI System, that allowed me to see various patterns from the person's birth date.

To test this even further, I would get the birth dates of the different basketball players, musicians, soccer players or other well known figures and see if I could make accurate observations about their lives, based on their birth date. The results were astonishing and I referred to them in my first book, 'Grasshopping through Time' where I referred to this particular pattern of high stress times as the 'Wisdom Star'.

In the present book, I take this to a whole new level and, as part of that, I have found a new way to visualise this on paper. In my first book, I used a square and a grid to show the relationship between the numbers and the patterns in the 9 Star Ki system, as is the norm. Over the last fifteen years as I got deeper into doing the research for the contextual winning field, an imprint from my childhood kept forming in my mind.

There was a gentleman by the name of Bertie Marshall who is known in Trinidad as the Master Innovator of the steel pan - or the steel drum as we refer to it in the UK. It was his research and his work that took it to where it is today.

When I was a child growing up in Belmont Valley Road, I saw him when he came to tune some pans in the yard opposite to where I lived. He would take an ordinary oil drum and using heat and a hammer would transform it magically into a tuned instrument. An amazing creation, that triggered an entire musical genre that spread around the world.

When you looked down at a finished pan, you could see that the flat top of the oil drum had been transformed into a concave shape, divided into segments each of which would produce a different note when struck.

It was this image of the circle, divided into segments, that inspired me to change the way I visualised the numbers and the patterns in the 9 Star Ki system.

For me, each number resonates at a different frequency, in just the same way that the segment of a pan sounded a note. It was natural that they should be represented in the same layout.

This is a living experience which I'm seeking to share with people, to bring about a sense of harmony in their life, a sense of elegance, a sense of joy, a sense of being in command when dealing with time and in dealing with their circumstances in life. So I felt this has to be a circle, it can no longer be a box or a square.

I was fortunate to have been instilled from an early age with a fascination and a love of number and patterns, and I do understand that for many people, numbers are a source of stress. To get the full benefit from my book, you will need to put that feeling to one side and to look at numbers in an entirely new and joyful way. Once you discover your patterns, so many things will start to make sense for you - about you, your habits and how you live and experience life.

OBSERVING LIFE AND ASKING QUESTIONS

A CHILDHOOD PARADOX

When I was a young boy in Trinidad, I remember being amazed and intrigued during school chemistry classes by the changes in the colour and properties of liquids when they were mixed with other liquids. Mr. Downer, the chemistry teacher at St. Mary's College, would always explain why these changes took place, and encouraged us to ask questions about things happening around us. "You need to be questioning what you are observing in order to get clarity", he would say.

This dichotomy between the empirical world of science and an almost shamanic view of signs and portents from the appearance of phenomena in the world of nature is still a strong presence in my life right up to the present day.

This is a daily dance that occupies my inner dialogue with myself of what I am experiencing. In a way I see the stream of life that is in front of me as an ongoing communication that is asking me to seek relevance to its messages. The dynamics of this dancing allowed me to write my first book on this subject, "Grasshopping Through Time".

However, during the past decade or more, this dichotomy has become even more pronounced for me, to the point where simply observing events in the world has become more important than unearthing any "reasons why".

As this process has become more profound in the last years, **CONTEXTUAL WINNING** is what has arisen. Of course, along the way as I explored and shared some of these observations with some people, a constant concern to them was the following:

NOT BEING TAKEN SERIOUSLY

Sometimes, when I sought feedback and advice from peers or mentors in the recent past about certain aspects of my work, they ask me questions.

For example: "Do you expect to be taken seriously when you state that Sir Winston Churchill's black hat, black suit and black umbrella have any relationship to his capacities as a leader?"

Or "Are you saying that Charlie Chaplin's genius was influenced in a positive way by the colour of HIS clothes and umbrella as well?"

Or "Are you claiming that the capacity and prowess of these people is linked in some strange way to something which you are calling the Wisdom Star? What have you been smoking? Or have you been drinking the wrong Kool-Aid?"

I am fully aware that from the perspective of the modern world, with its love of information technology and its worship of The Scientific Method, the point of view that I am putting forward does seem a little delusional: OK, strike that: a whole **bunch** delusional.

However, I would like to invite you to step out of the consensual viewpoint for a moment, suspend your disbelief and come and explore something with me...let's start right here.

CHAPTER 1

The Wisdom Star,
and how it became the contextual winning field

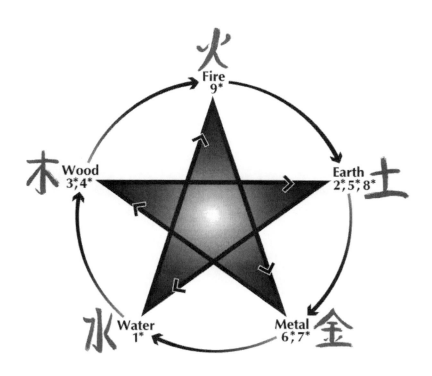

Every great dream begins
with a dreamer.
Always remember,
you have within you
the strength, the patience,
and the passion to
reach for the stars
to change the world.

Harriet Tubman

CHAPTER 1
The Wisdom Star, and how it became the contextual winning field

FROM WISDOM STAR TO CONTEXTUAL WINNING

The journey of observing my students, patients and clients over many decades using the compass of the Oriental Astrology system of 9 Star Ki, and its foundation within the 5 Elements, has allowed me to see certain consistent patterns arising. I could not help but wonder if these same patterns were accurate for famous world personalities in different fields, for example sports, business, politics, entertainment etc. When I did my homework, and realized that the same patterns WERE arising within these famous people's lives, it led me to discern something that I named the Wisdom Star.

I described this in Chapter 9 of my book "Grasshopping Through Time".

I quote from the opening paragraph of chapter 9 of that book: "One of the beautiful things about the 9 Star Ki system is that you can easily forecast times of high stress, times of easy flow and times when your energetic quality tends to be insensitive to your circumstances. This chapter focuses on managing the times of high stress."

The impact of STRESS, which is ever constant in our lives, clearly shows that people who have the capacity to excel and deliver peak performances in stressful situations would be leaders and icons in ventures they undertook.

Since writing that first book, with its single chapter on the Wisdom Star, I have dug deeper into these patterns.

WHAT IS THE WISDOM STAR?

To get an answer to this, we need to look at the matrix of what the 9 Star Ki System of Astrology is about. Basically, from your date of birth you are able to obtain what is termed Your Adult Star number and your Child Star number. This you get from a 9 Star Ki Calendar. These two star numbers are the core foundation of the 9 Star Ki Astrology System.

However, here I'm taking the ancient Oriental system of 9 Star Ki and creating a whole new paradigm, totally based on the two key pillars of my approach to observation of the world around me. These pillars are the principle of 5 Elements and their interaction, along with the qualities of the 9 Stars from the 9 Star Ki system. I'm taking a very deep look into the lives and actions of self-actualized individuals, and I've found "a DNA pattern", for want of a better term, that points to what this new book is about.

CONTEXTUAL WINNING FIELD

I'm going to explore not only what we see on the surface with people, I'm going to tune you in to "The Iceberg Factor", what is below the surface of human beings. We're going to look at their "operating system" and the "hardware" and "software" that makes them tick, to use computer jargon, terminology that fits so neatly into the digital world.

However, and this is a core aspect of my approach, I am most certainly not embracing the digital world, as I view it as a coffin, a box we put ourselves into, and then walk around with this coffin over our heads as we text ourselves through life.

The biggest shock for traditional 9 Star Ki exponents and aficionados will be that I now have my 9 Star Ki charts in a circle. Why? Well, these charts are **mandalas**, and they have a biological basis as the system is based on the elements of life, the seasons, the cosmology of our lives on planet earth, and is not a conceptual mental construct, which has no connection with life.

4	9	2
3	5	7
8	1	6

Traditional, "coffin"-style 9 Ki Square

9 Star Ki charts are a **snapshot of life**.

All aspects of chi, Ki, prana, Q'i, living energy, are spirals and/or circles.

None are a box or a square or rectangle.

None are coffins.

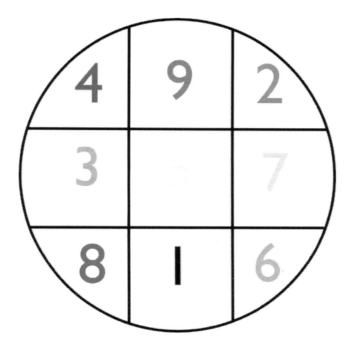

Mandala-style, vibrant living snapshot 9 Ki Circle

What I observed decades ago was when these two star numbers (Adult number and Child number) are separated by a Star Number in the centre of the 9 Star Ki Square/circle, also termed the Lo Shu square (now perhaps the Lo Shu Circle), you then had a star number that most frequently highlighted a high stress time in a person's life. I also observed that such a time can trigger a peak creative period for an individual and that many of the trailblazers in the world had major ingenious actions when this was the case. I call this star that is at the centre of their opposing star numbers the Wisdom Star, and it is also the CONTEXTUAL WINNING star.

WHY CONTEXTUAL WINNING

I discovered that individuals who were leaders, masters and doyennes in their chosen field frequently achieved dominant breakthroughs in their particular Contextual Winning Time.

They lived their lives, unconsciously, but with very clear and diligent focus in their field of endeavor, applying a **"winning context"** for their creative calling.

In the following chapters l point out **the dynamics of these empowering patterns which define CONTEXTUAL WINNING.**

The activation of the inherent energy and qualities of the Wisdom Star is what moves it into the CONTEXTUAL WINNING expression. These unconscious masters were doing this constantly with their creative gift and skill.

You, the reader of this book, are now in possession of what this skill set is about and how to use it.

It is much more than a map, as I am going to walk with you in a very personal way to show you how, if you so wish, can also have access to these "Contextual Winning Templates" to celebrate the creative fire that is the essence of who you are.

A core source of inspiration in the writing of Contextual Winning for me has been an iconic figure from my home country, Trinidad and Tobago, Mr Bertie Marshall. In a way, the inspiration from his innovative spirit and quiet creative genius was a seed that was planted in my mind when I saw him do his work when I was a young boy in Belmont, my hometown.

A SILENT IMPRINT THAT RIPENED

This story is a silent imprint that I experienced in my early teen years, when the master innovator of the steel pan Bertie Marshall came to the steel band yard. This was opposite my home in Belmont Valley Road in Port of Spain where he was cutting, tuning and creating musical instruments from 45 gallon oil drums.

Bertie Marshall walked into the yard about 9 one morning, where I had gone to play with some of my neighborhood friends. Bertie had this bag on his shoulder with his tools - he said nothing, and went to the pans that had been left in the yard for him to cut and tune. The pounding of the drums started along with the cutting, all in silence with Mr. Marshall. At this stage, I went and sat on the front steps of the house in the yard and just watched. In a way taken into another world of creation, bringing a being into life.

My friends drifted away and although it was a big yard somehow Mr. Marshall and his actions and intent were occupying the whole yard. Bertie Marshall was pregnant with the many pans in the yard. Wood was gathered, and a fire was lit: then he put a pan on the fire and Mr. Marshall's eyes became those of an eagle, ready to pounce on the right moment when he would pull the pan off and pour water onto it. Another level of pounding began, at that stage, of a very different quality. This pounding was extremely subtle, and his hammer started to explore many areas of that dented pan with a steel pan stick, then his hammer. Sometimes he would bring out something that looked like a big spanner to hit it in a certain way or reverse the hammer to the rounded ball side to hit it. I had to be conscious of the time, as at 11.15, or at the latest 11.30, I had to start heading home, otherwise I would start hearing REX!!!! from my mother's voice and if that was the case that meant I would have to receive answers from my mother with my skin and not my ears, as my parents had a law that between 11.30 a.m. and 1 p.m. I had to be home, unless the neighbors invited me for lunch. Very timidly, I asked Mr. Marshall "Mister, can you tell me the time please?"

"Twenty past eleven" Mr. Marshall answered. I said "Thank you Mister, ah coming back after lunch." "Ok" he said. One needs to remember that I did not know the name of this man, who had become pregnant with the steel drums in the yard. Yet, he was working with a total focus on bringing these drums into being, starting a life as a musical instrument. It was only a few years later, when I was in the steelband yard one early evening before the band started to practice, that Bertie Marshall showed up to tune some pans and his name was mentioned. Again, the silent quality was ever-present with the man, he gave brief smiles and hellos to those around and took that special tool bag of his off his shoulder and immediately started to tune some pans for the evening practice.

When I returned after lunch, I observed that there was an empty Solo bottle on the step, and a small paper bag with the remains of some snacks in it, that Mr. Marshall seemed to have had for his lunch. These circular instruments became living musical entities under the hands of midwife, master pan cutter and tuner Mr. Bertie Marshall.

The sounds of those instruments are still resonating inside of me more than fifty years later. They have remained alive in my being all these decades. In that silent way of Mr. Bertie Marshall, the silence of the sound of his pounding those drums, persistently, diligently, is a gentle echo that remains as a core inspiration in my life.

These Contextual Winning charts are life beings on the page, that echo throughout our lives. They are the context for our lives and if we can engage with them like Mr. Bertie Marshall did with the pans, then the sounds of our lives will inspire us and inspire others and bring a new platform for spontaneity, harmony and elegant self-expression to who we are as human beings.

The inherent qualities that are present with the Wisdom Star become CONTEXTUAL WINNING when these core qualities come alive in people. Such people are then operating with their CONTEXTUAL WINNING Field.

When this happens the seed of the Wisdom Star has become a flourishing tree with roots, a trunk, branches, leaves, blossoms, fruits.

In the book, you, the reader, will learn how to allow the seed of your essence to become a flourishing tree.

My "How To" menu will let you know the things to **DO** and the things to **AVOID**, along with how to achieve this.

Contextual Winning gives you **Clear Indicators** that tell you when your lifestyle is in a place of Imbalance as it relates to your personal Contextual Winning Field. It even goes further, to indicate very clear signals that you are in a danger zone with how you are operating in life.

Many of my clients have come to view their relationship with their Contextual Winning Field as an ever-present Guardian Angel that offers them specific guidance for accomplishing their dreams and goals.

Interestingly, in the book CONTEXTUAL WINNING you get to know what you need to do to cultivate a winning relationship with your CONTEXTUAL WINNING Field.

I do not want you to believe
what I've written here.
I really want you to engage with it
in a way that it becomes practical
and that it makes a difference
in your life.

Making a difference in your life
is what this book is about.
Your contextual winning field can
do that for you as you embrace it
and discover things with it.

Rex

CHAPTER 2

What is my context for winning?

THE ADULT STAR NUMBER CHART

year	#	year	#	year	#	year	#	year	#	year	#	year	#	year	#	year	#	year	#
1756	1	1801	1	1846	1	1891	1	1936	1	1981	1	2026	1	2071	1	2116	1	2161	1
1757	9	1802	9	1847	9	1892	9	1937	9	1982	9	2027	9	2072	9	2117	9	2162	9
1758	8	1803	8	1848	8	1893	8	1938	8	1983	8	2028	8	2073	8	2118	8	2163	8
1759	7	1804	7	1849	7	1894	7	1939	7	1984	7	2029	7	2074	7	2119	7	2164	7
1760	6	1805	6	1850	6	1895	6	1940	6	1985	6	2030	6	2075	6	2120	6	2165	6
1761	5	1806	5	1851	5	1896	5	1941	5	1986	5	2031	5	2076	5	2121	5	2166	5
1762	4	1807	4	1852	4	1897	4	1942	4	1987	4	2032	4	2077	4	2122	4	2167	4
1763	3	1808	3	1853	3	1898	3	1943	3	1988	3	2033	3	2078	3	2123	3	2168	3
1764	2	1809	2	1854	2	1899	2	1944	2	1989	2	2034	2	2079	2	2124	2	2169	2
1765	1	1810	1	1855	1	1900	1	1945	1	1990	1	2035	1	2080	1	2125	1	2170	1
1766	9	1811	9	1856	9	1901	9	1946	9	1991	9	2036	9	2081	9	2126	9	2171	9
1767	8	1812	8	1857	8	1902	8	1947	8	1992	8	2037	8	2082	8	2127	8	2172	8
1768	7	1813	7	1858	7	1903	7	1948	7	1993	7	2038	7	2083	7	2128	7	2173	7
1769	6	1814	6	1859	6	1904	6	1949	6	1994	6	2039	6	2084	6	2129	6	2174	6
1770	5	1815	5	1860	5	1905	5	1950	5	1995	5	2040	5	2085	5	2130	5	2175	5
1771	4	1816	4	1861	4	1906	4	1951	4	1996	4	2041	4	2086	4	2131	4	2176	4
1772	3	1817	3	1862	3	1907	3	1952	3	1997	3	2042	3	2087	3	2132	3	2177	3
1773	2	1818	2	1863	2	1908	2	1953	2	1998	2	2043	2	2088	2	2133	2	2178	2
1774	1	1819	1	1864	1	1909	1	1954	1	1999	1	2044	1	2089	1	2134	1	2179	1
1775	9	1820	9	1865	9	1910	9	1955	9	2000	9	2045	9	2090	9	2135	9	2180	9
1776	8	1821	8	1866	8	1911	8	1956	8	2001	8	2046	8	2091	8	2136	8	2181	8
1777	7	1822	7	1867	7	1912	7	1957	7	2002	7	2047	7	2092	7	2137	7	2182	7
1778	6	1823	6	1868	6	1913	6	1958	6	2003	6	2048	6	2093	6	2138	6	2183	6
1779	5	1824	5	1869	5	1914	5	1959	5	2004	5	2049	5	2094	5	2139	5	2184	5
1780	4	1825	4	1870	4	1915	4	1960	4	2005	4	2050	4	2095	4	2140	4	2185	4
1781	3	1826	3	1871	3	1916	3	1961	3	2006	3	2051	3	2096	3	2141	3	2186	3
1782	2	1827	2	1872	2	1917	2	1962	2	2007	2	2052	2	2097	2	2142	2	2187	2
1783	1	1828	1	1873	1	1918	1	1963	1	2008	1	2053	1	2098	1	2143	1	2188	1
1784	9	1829	9	1874	9	1919	9	1964	9	2009	9	2054	9	2099	9	2144	9	2189	9
1785	8	1830	8	1875	8	1920	8	1965	8	2010	8	2055	8	2100	8	2145	8	2190	8
1786	7	1831	7	1876	7	1921	7	1966	7	2011	7	2056	7	2101	7	2146	7	2191	7
1787	6	1832	6	1877	6	1922	6	1967	6	2012	6	2057	6	2102	6	2147	6	2192	6
1788	5	1833	5	1878	5	1923	5	1968	5	2013	5	2058	5	2103	5	2148	5	2193	5
1789	4	1834	4	1879	4	1924	4	1969	4	2014	4	2059	4	2104	4	2149	4	2194	4
1790	3	1835	3	1880	3	1925	3	1970	3	2015	3	2060	3	2105	3	2150	3	2195	3
1791	2	1836	2	1881	2	1926	2	1971	2	2016	2	2061	2	2106	2	2151	2	2196	2
1792	1	1837	1	1882	1	1927	1	1972	1	2017	1	2062	1	2107	1	2152	1	2197	1
1793	9	1838	9	1883	9	1928	9	1973	9	2018	9	2063	9	2108	9	2153	9	2198	9
1794	8	1839	8	1884	8	1929	8	1974	8	2019	8	2064	8	2109	8	2154	8	2199	8
1795	7	1840	7	1885	7	1930	7	1975	7	2020	7	2065	7	2110	7	2155	7	2200	7
1796	6	1841	6	1886	6	1931	6	1976	6	2021	6	2066	6	2111	6	2156	6	2201	6
1797	5	1842	5	1887	5	1932	5	1977	5	2022	5	2067	5	2112	5	2157	5	2202	5
1798	4	1843	4	1888	4	1933	4	1978	4	2023	4	2068	4	2113	4	2158	4	2203	4
1799	3	1844	3	1889	3	1934	3	1979	3	2024	3	2069	3	2114	3	2159	3	2204	3
1800	2	1845	2	1890	2	1935	2	1980	2	2025	2	2070	2	2115	2	2160	2	2205	2

CHAPTER 2
What is my context for winning?

Your context happens by pulling back for a while from the hustle and bustle of life and with your mind consciously changing gears and giving yourself permission to connect with Your Contextual Winning Field. You first need to identify it.
Here is how that is done.

SO WHAT IS MY CONTEXTUAL WINNING FIELD?

Your Contextual Winning Field is the centre point of the Lo Shu square when your Child Star number and your Adult Star number are opposite each other across the square. To discover when that is, you need to know your Adult Star number. Look in the Adult Star number chart. I have listed it here from 1756 to 2205.

REMEMBER THAT THE ADULT STAR NUMBER BEGINS ON FEBRUARY 4th AND ENDS ON FEBRUARY 3rd OF THE FOLLOWING YEAR.

For instance, if you were born January 10 1973, the year you need to look at is 1972 in order to discover your Adult Star number.

THE CHILD STAR NUMBER CHART

ADULT STAR →	1	2	3	4	5	6	7	8	9
February 4 - March 5	8	2	5	8	2	5	8	2	5
March 6 - April 4	7	1	4	7	1	4	7	1	4
April 5 - May 5	6	9	3	6	9	3	6	9	3
May 6 - June 5	5	8	2	5	8	2	5	8	2
June 6 - July 7	4	7	1	4	7	1	4	7	1
July 8 - August 7	3	6	9	3	6	9	3	6	9
August 8 - September 7	2	5	8	2	5	8	2	5	8
September 8 - October 8	1	4	7	1	4	7	1	4	7
October 9 - November 7	9	3	6	9	3	6	9	3	6
November 8 - December 8	8	2	5	8	2	5	8	2	5
December 9 - January 5	7	1	4	7	1	4	7	1	4
January 6 - February 3	6	9	3	6	9	3	6	9	3

To discover your Child Star number, use the Child Star chart listed on the facing page.

Go across the top of the chart and identify your Adult Star number, then go down the column of your Adult Star to the month when your birthday is. Where the columns intersect gives you the Child Star of the month in which you were born.

Example 1 If your birthday is 1 June 1976, your Adult Star number is 6. Find the 6 at the top of the chart, then find the row that is May 6–June 5. Where the 6 column and the May 6-June 5 row intersect is the number 2. Therefore, your Child Star number is 2.

Example 2 If your birthday is 19 Dec. 1965, your Adult Star number is 8. Find the 8 at the top of the chart, then find the row that is Dec. 9–Jan. 5. Where the 8 column and the Dec. 9–Jan.5 row intersect is the number 1. Therefore, your Child Star number is 1.

IMPORTANT INFORMATION FOR DOUBLE 5 EARTH STAR PEOPLE

I have found that you need to look at the moon phases in order to gain a clearer picture of whether the double 5 Earth Star person will take on the feminine number 2 Earth Star aspect or the masculine number 8 Earth Star aspect, regardless of the individual's physical gender.

This is determined by the moons' aspect at the time of birth. Please note that a waxing/growing/expanding moon at the time of birth gives a feminine expression to the double 5 Earth Star, thus changing it to a double 2 Earth Star. In this scenario, the person's Contextual Winning Field will be 8 Earth

A waning/contracting/retreating moon at the time of birth gives a masculine expression to the double 5 Earth Star personality, thus shifting it to a double 8 Earth Star. In this case, the person's Contextual Winning Field will be 2 Earth.

I append below the moon phase charts for the relevant months between 1806 and 2049.

THE DOUBLE 5 STAR MOON PHASE CHART

YEAR	DATE	PHASE	STAR	YEAR	DATE	PHASE	STAR
1806	8.8 - 14.8	Waning	8 Earth	1932	8.8 - 16.8	Waxing	2 Earth
	15.8 - 29.8	Waxing	2 Earth		17.8 - 31.8	Waning	8 Earth
	30.8 - 7.9	Waning	8 Earth		1.9 - 7.9	Waxing	2 Earth
1815	8.8 - 20.8	Waxing	2 Earth	1941	8.8 - 22.8	Waning	8 Earth
	21.8 - 3.9	Waning	8 Earth		23.8 - 5.9	Waxing	2 Earth
	4.9 - 7.9	Waxing	2 Earth		6.9 - 7.9	Waning	8 Earth
1824	8.8 - 9.8	Waxing	2 Earth	1950	8.8 - 13.8	Waning	8 Earth
	10.8 - 24.8	Waning	8 Earth		14.8 - 27.8	Waxing	2 Earth
	25.8 - 7.9	Waxing	2 Earth		28.8 - 7.9	Waning	8 Earth
1833	8.8 - 15.8	Waning	8 Earth	1959	8.8 - 18.8	Waxing	2 Earth
	16.8 - 30.8	Waxing	2 Earth		19.8 - 3.9	Waning	8 Earth
	31.8 - 7.9	Waning	8 Earth		4.9 - 7.9	Waxing	2 Earth
1842	8.8 - 21.8	Waxing	2 Earth	1968	8.8 - 15.8	Waxing	2 Earth
	22.8 - 4.9	Waning	8 Earth		16.8 - 30.8	Waning	8 Earth
	5.9 - 7.9	Waxing	2 Earth		31.8 - 7.9	Waxing	2 Earth
1851	8.8 - 11.8	Waxing	2 Earth	1977	8.8 - 23.8	Waning	8 Earth
	12.8 - 26.8	Waning	8 Earth		24.8 - 6-9	Waxing	2 Earth
	27.8 - 7.9	Waxing	2 Earth		7.9	Waning	8 Earth
1860	8.8 - 16.8	Waning	8 Earth	1986	8.8 - 19.8	Waxing	2 Earth
	17.8 - 31.8	Waxing	2 Earth		20.8 - 4.9	Waning	8 Earth
	1.9 - 7.9	Waning	8 Earth		5.9 - 7.9	Waxing	2 Earth
1869	8.8 - 21.8	Waxing	2 Earth	1995	8.8 - 10.8	Waxing	2 Earth
	22.8 - 4.9	Waning	8 Earth		11.8 - 26.8	Waning	8 Earth
	5.9 - 7.9	Waxing	2 Earth		27.8 - 7.9	Waxing	2 Earth
1878	8.8 - 13.8	Waxing	2 Earth	2004	8.8 - 23.8	Waning	8 Earth
	14.8 - 28.8	Waning	8 Earth		24.8 - 7.9	Waxing	2 Earth
	29.8 - 7.9	Waxing	2 Earth	2013	8.8 - 14.8	Waning	8 Earth
1887	8.8 - 19.8	Waning	8 Earth		15.8 - 28.8	Waxing	2 Earth
	20.8 - 2.9	Waxing	2 Earth		29.8 - 7.9	Waning	8 Earth
	3.9 - 7.9	Waning	8 Earth	2022	8.8 - 12.8	Waxing	2 Earth
1896	8.8 - 9.8	Waning	8 Earth		13.8 - 27.8	Waning	8 Earth
	10.8 - 23.8	Waxing	2 Earth		28.8 - 7.9	Waxing	2 Earth
	24.8 - 7.9	Waning	8 Earth	2031	8.8 - 18.8	Waning	8 Earth
1905	8.8 - 15.8	Waxing	2 Earth		19.8 - 1.9	Waxing	2 Earth
	16.8 - 30.8	Waning	8 Earth		2.9 - 7.9	Waning	8 Earth
	31.8 - 7.9	Waxing	2 Earth	2040	8.8	Waning	8 Earth
1914	8.8 - 21.8	Waning	8 Earth		9.8 - 22.8	Waxing	2 Earth
	22.8 - 4.9	Waxing	2 Earth		23.8 - 6.9	Waning	8 Earth
	5.9 - 7.9	Waning	8 Earth		7.9	Waxing	2 Earth
1923	8.8 - 12.8	Waning	8 Earth	2049	8.8 - 13.8	Waxing	2 Earth
	13.8 - 26.8	Waxing	2 Earth		14.8 - 28.8	Waning	8 Earth
	27.8 - 7.9	Waning	8 Earth		29.8 - 7.9	Waxing	2 Earth

The MOON PHASE CHART

Having now discovered both your Adult Star Number and your Child Star number, you can take a look at the Contextual Winning Field Chart. The first number listed is your Adult Star number, and the Second number is your Child Star number. The number that follows these is your CONTEXTUAL WINNING FIELD NUMBER.

THE CONTEXTUAL WINNING FIELD CHART

ADULT STAR	CHILD STAR	CWF	ADULT STAR	CHILD STAR	CWF
1	1	6 METAL	6	1	8 EARTH
1	2	6 METAL	6	2	4 WOOD
1	3	2 EARTH	6	3	9 FIRE
1	4	7 METAL	6	4	5 EARTH
1	6	8 EARTH	6	6	7 METAL
1	7	4 WOOD	6	7	2 EARTH
1	8	9 FIRE	6	8	7 METAL
1	9	5 EARTH	6	9	3 WOOD
2	1	6 METAL	7	1	4 WOOD
2	2	8 EARTH	7	2	9 FIRE
2	3	7 METAL	7	3	5 EARTH
2	4	3 WOOD	7	4	1 WATER
2	6	4 WOOD	7	6	2 EARTH
2	7	9 FIRE	7	7	9 FIRE
2	8	5 EARTH	7	8	3 WOOD
2	9	1 WATER	7	9	8 EARTH
3	1	2 EARTH	8	1	9 FIRE
3	2	7 METAL	8	2	5 EARTH
3	3	1 WATER	8	3	1 WATER
3	4	8 EARTH	8	4	6 METAL
3	6	9 FIRE	8	6	7 METAL
3	7	5 EARTH	8	7	3 WOOD
3	8	1 WATER	8	8	2 EARTH
3	9	6 METAL	8	9	4 WOOD
4	1	7 METAL	9	1	5 EARTH
4	2	3 WOOD	9	2	1 WATER
4	3	8 EARTH	9	3	6 METAL
4	4	3 WOOD	9	4	2 EARTH
4	6	5 EARTH	9	6	3 WOOD
4	7	1 WATER	9	7	8 EARTH
4	8	6 METAL	9	8	4 WOOD
4	9	2 EARTH	9	9	4 WOOD

Now that you have your Contextual Winning Field number you are now ready to discover what your Contextual Winning Field is about.
Have a look.

1 WATER CONTEXTUAL WINNING FIELD

Your 1 Water Contextual Field is manifesting when the following are happening:

1. OPERATING WITH CONFIDENCE IN THE INTANGIBLE DIMENSION OF LIFE

2. BEING AN IMAGINATIVE CREATOR

3. BEING A SKILLFUL MASS COMMUNICATOR

4. BEING A PERSEVERING VISIONARY

5. ENJOYING SEEMINGLY EFFORTLESS ARTISTIC EXPRESSION

Smooth flowing waterfall ever present

Forgetting and being lost happens yet never water to me.

Deep blue waters pour into my present

Embracing them clarity, conviction to be.

Water touching whatever present

Endless Ganges persists blessing all to be.

Effortless, elegant, never-ending

2 EARTH CONTEXTUAL WINNING FIELD

Your 2 Earth Contextual Winning Field is manifesting when the following are happening:

1. HAVE THE CAPACITY TO BE INSPIRED FROM THE SPIRITUAL DIMENSION

2. EXHIBIT A SINCERE CONCERN FOR HUMANITY

3. BEING AN ICONIC IMAGE CREATOR

4. ENJOYING THE CAPACITY TO OPENLY SHARE YOUR LIFE

5. HAVING THE ABILITY TO RECREATE YOUR SELF

Orange honey-suckled flower wafting inspiration

Mouth waters take me to NOW

Now grounds me to serve

Serve!

Orange flower transforms Now

Now arises in public, heads turn

Wafting honeysuckle keeps enchanting public zone.

3 WOOD CONTEXTUAL WINNING FIELD

Your 3 Wood Contextual Winning Field is manifesting when the following are happening:

1. BEING A HIGH RISK TAKER

2. SPURN RIGID FORMS OF EXPRESSION

3. CHALLENGE ORTHODOXY

4. TRAVELLING BEYOND YOUR HORIZONS

5. HELP UNFOLD NEW SOCIAL AND POLITICAL RESPONSES

Your long green bamboo, stretches to infinity.

Ignoring what went before

Lightening searcher embracing thunder

Green sprouts of spring, bamboo father at core

Flourishing forever

Eyes sparkle with resilience, flexibility forever

4 WOOD CONTEXTUAL WINNING FIELD

Your 4 Wood Contextual Field is manifesting when the following are happening:

1. BE SKILLFUL AT CREATING NEW POSSIBILITIES

2. BE A COMMUNICATOR OF EPIC PROPORTIONS

3. EXPERIENCE TRANSFORMING YOUR LIFE

4. BE IN PERSISTENT SEARCH FOR DEEP INNER MEANING

5. DEEP RELATIONSHIP WITH TRADITIONAL VALUES

6. PRACTICE IN DEPTH NOTE-TAKING IN GREAT DETAIL

Wind blows turquoise glistening leaves symphony arises

Mesmerised; jaw drops, hips sway from origin

What's that WISSS who is listening claps arises

Honouring wind seeking its origins

Missing not a sound moment by moment

Identifying facts discovering wind origins

5 EARTH CONTEXTUAL WINNING FIELD

Your 5 Earth Contextual Winning Field is manifesting when the following are happening:

1. BRING OUT THE BEST IN OTHERS

2. BE SOCIAL REFORMERS

3. HAVE A TIMELESS QUALITY OF EXPRESSION

4. EXPRESS A NEW VISION, A NEW POSSIBILITY

5. ARE DILIGENT IN APPLICATION

Yellow Rose holds timeless dewdrop

Garden changes, eyes open, new realization

Supreme expression of possibilities manifest

Enrollment occurs stability anchored

Dewdrop stains imagination endlessly

6 METAL CONTEXTUAL WINNING FIELD

Your 6 Metal Contextual Winning Field is manifesting when the following are happening:

1. BEING SINGLE MINDED AND PERSISTENT

2. HONORING ETHICAL PURSUITS

3. HAVING AN ALL-PERVASIVE INFLUENCE ON YOUR GENRE

4. PRESENT A TRANSCENDENTAL QUALITY IN ARTISTIC EXPRESSION

5. BE AN ICONIC AND INIMITABLE PERFORMER

White waves foam at feet sinking white sand

Keep rolling back shadow less

Evening dusk light envelops sky as space and openness stretches horizon

Lower belly sighs AH, as spaciousness hugs you.

7 METAL CONTEXTUAL WINNING FIELD

Your 7 Metal Contextual Winning Field is manifesting when the following are happening:

1. BE A SKILLFUL MARKETER

2. BE A HUMAN RIGHTS ACTIVIST AND PROMOTER

3. BE A STRUCTURAL REFORMER

4. BEING AN EXPONENT OF ENTERTAINMENT SKILLS

5. BE AN EFFICIENT ORGANIZER AND ADMINISTRATOR

Sunset lights the sky pure elegance captures you.

Sun appears as orb of white light.

A demanding breath taking sunset shared righteously

Rays of sunset now touches all homes

As breath deepens, goose bumps rejoicing spread joy

8 EARTH CONTEXTUAL WINNING FIELD

Your 8 Earth Contextual Winning Field is manifesting when the following are happening:

1. TRANSFORMING YOUR ESSENCE

2. BE AN AUTHENTIC SEEKER

3. BE TENACIOUS

4. BEING READY TO TAKE A STAND

5. BE A CREATOR OF MONUMENTAL ARTISTIC CREATIONS

Amber mountain brings awe, unwavering

Ever-present observer, a navel,

Amber mountain observing

Always enduring

Amber bites mountain alchemy unfolds

9 FIRE CONTEXTUAL WINNING FIELD

Your 9 Fire Contextual Winning Field is manifesting when the following are happening:

1. BE DOMINANT LEADER IN YOUR CHOSEN FIELD

2. ENJOY WORKING UP A SWEAT

3. BE STRONGLY PASSIONATE ABOUT YOUR VIEWPOINTS AND EXPRESSIONS

4. BE CONSUMED BY WHAT YOU DO

5. BE A PIONEER

6. ENJOY MAKING THINGS VISUAL

Burning log, deep red glow shines forth

Intense revelation passionately pours forth

Energy flows from gut through heart.

Not seen before a torn celebrating heart

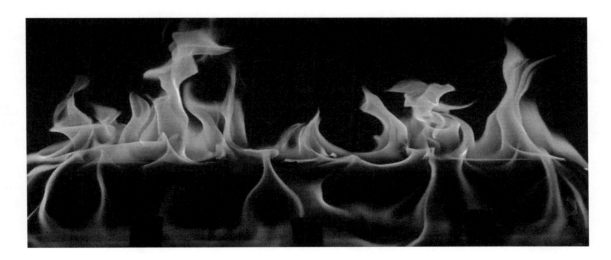

Science has tried to

assume a monopoly -

or, rather, a tyranny -

over our understanding

of the world around us ...

We are only now beginning

to understand the disastrous

results of this outlook.

Prince Charles

CHAPTER 3

How to manifest your contextual winning field

"The five elements pervade every

aspect of physical experience,

therefore the condition of

the elements as they change

under seasonal influences

is reflected internally."

Dr. Yeshi Donden:
Health Through Balance.

CHAPTER 3
How to manifest your contextual winning field

Your Contextual Winning Field is something that you will fall in love with when you discover its uplifting qualities.

When you discover the true nature of your field, you will say to yourself, "These are the qualities I need around me all the time. WELCOME, CONTEXTUAL WINNING FIELD, tell me more!"

The inherent qualities of your specific Contextual Winning Field arise from the energy of the 5 Elements, and these shift and change as the seasons do.

9 Fire Contextual Winning Field

You will find your Contextual Winning Field incredibly receptive to your approaches if you use the following strategies:

1. Use visualization daily to focus on what you want to create: develop your skills with this practice. Cultivate the habit of seeing things in great detail in your mind's eye, in Technicolor™.

2. Work with passion: permit no half-hearted efforts in your expression. Just go for it- no sitting back and hoping. Put your energy behind your efforts!

3. Look after your heart. Ensure that obesity doesn't even get a walk-on part in the movie of your life. If you are more than 10 kilos overweight, get rid of it: make this a priority. Foods that benefit the heart are corn, quinoa, amaranth, mushrooms (especially ling zhi mushrooms) watercress, dill, basil, chamomile.

4 . Work out enough to build up a good sweat each day. Stimulating your cardiovascular system creates a mental sharpness where your perceptions and responses are heightened.

5. Red hues and shades will support your best efforts. Be cautious with black and midnight blue, especially at peak times of creative expression.

6. Something else you could do is to rub your palms vigorously during the day from time to time so that heat develops between them. Then, place your palms over your closed eyes and allow a warm crimson glow to pour out from your heart along your arms into your eyes. Let this run for about 3 minutes, then sit in that heart space quietly with your palms on your lap and enjoy the glow. This will energize you and lift your spirits.

7. Massage the center of your chest on the sternum with some nutmeg oil in the evening before sleep. Be gentle, as this area can be tender. Persevere, and with a daily practice of two minutes at a time, in due course this discomfort will ease.

8. Be mindful of heat and hot conditions, as they can easily exhaust you. Obviously, your intake of water needs to be higher if you have to operate in these conditions. In addition, green tea can create a cooling quality, as can chrysanthemum tea. It is always best to have these within half an hour after eating.

9. Make your passions visual. Create pictures, images and sketches of your goals and dreams, and put these up so that you can see them during the day. Visualize yourself doing or accomplishing these things. Let your living space be an inspirational one that fires your imagination.

10. It is much better for things to be open and up-front during conflict resolution. Following these strategies will strengthen your connection to your Contextual Winning Field.

FAMOUS 9 FIRE CONTEXTUAL WINNING FIELD PERSONALITIES

Michael Jordan, Erwin Rommel, Jim Brown, Queen Victoria, Bob Marley, Burt Reynolds, Harry Belafonte, Jean Paul Sartre, Tom Cruise, Lena Horne, The Dalai Lama, Johnny Carson, Walter Cronkite, Joni Mitchell, Al Pacino, Norman Mailer, Tiger Woods, Joan Baez, Marvin Gaye, Helmut Kohl, Donna Summer, Steve Sondheim, Joss Stone, Sharon Osbourne, Jean-Claude Van Damme, Connie Francis, Andrew Young, Elton John, Maurice Ravel, Bobby McFerrin

Shiva Naipaul   Novelist   1/8   9CWF

Calypso Rose   6/3   9CWF

Edna Manley   Jamaican Sculptress   1/8   9CWF

Bernard Jordan American   preacher   2/7   9 CWF

Brother Valentino Calypsonian   2/7 9CWF

Paul Pogba footballer 7/7   9 CWF

Jack" Johnson boxer 8/1   9CWF

Les" Brown Motivational speaker 1/8   9CWF

Lady Gaga 8/1 9CWF

Jorge Paulo Lemann Swiss/Brazilian banker 7/2   9CWF

Ornette Coleman Jazz musician 7/7   9CWF

 Mamphela Ramphele   South African politician 8/1   9CWF

Dr. Clark American Baptist preacher 8/1   9 CWF

Lord Kitchener Calypsonian 6/3 9CWF

Drupatee Ramgoonai Soca/chutney singer 1/8   9CWF

Sundar Popo Chutney singer 3/6   9CWF

8 Earth Contextual Winning Field

You will find your Contextual Winning Field incredibly receptive to your approaches if you use the following strategies:

1. Research, check, go deeper with your projects.
Seek a foundation that is truly solid, one that you have discovered for yourself.
Find your own baseline, and then develop your style and approach from this: avoid copying others.

2. Celebrate being a loner, because in many ways you are just not a team player. It's not that you have anything against teams: however, only your own searches and explorations can take you into uncharted territories, and having to explain this to others depletes you of energy which could be better utilized in developing your creative efforts.

3. Nourish your spleen. Excellent foods for the spleen are corn, millet, rye, aduki beans, turnips, scallions, kohlrabi, ginger, garbanzo beans, nutmeg, black cardamom and anchovies.

4. One great exercise for 8 Earth Contextual Winning Fields is bouncing on a rebounder. Bounce in the morning before your breakfast. Start with 5 minutes of bouncing and build up to 20 minutes over a 6-week period. Women can also get into belly dancing, if they want to. Both of these activities are a superb workout for the lymph system and the spleen.

5 Amber and golden hues and shades will support your best efforts. Be cautious with green, especially during peak times of creative expression.

6. Massage your navel 108 times in a clockwise direction. Essential oil of fennel would be supportive with this practice. This creates great stimulus for the lymph system, which is so important for 8 Contextual Winning Field personalities.

Do persevere with this, as it can often be the most important magic wand for all 8 Earth Contextual Winning Field personalities.

7. Humidity and dampness will sabotage your best efforts. If you are working under such conditions, it is important for you to avoid the following foods: dairy items, peanuts, bananas, deep fried foods, coffee, alcohol,sugary or sweet items and dishes that create mucous and phlegm in the body.

Excellent foods that can overcome dampness are celery, kohlrabi, turnips, scallions, amaranth, corn, rye, aduki beans and pumpkins, pumpkin seeds, pumpkin seed butter, sesame seeds.

Sitting for long periods can contribute to stagnation, which can in turn contribute to dampness. If you are stuck in front of a computer for long periods, taking a brisk walk every three hours or so is an important way of keeping your creative juices flowing.

In addition, lotus root tea will cut through mucous and dampness in your system like a hot knife through butter.

8. Items suggestive of study and research in the living space will always enroll 8 Earth Contextual Winning Field personalities to give of their best. A tidy shelf of books with a well-lit desk invokes the energy of the researcher who is willing to persevere in their task.

Following these strategies will strengthen your connection to your Contextual Winning Field.

FAMOUS 8 EARTH CONTEXTUAL WINNING FIELD PERSONALITIES

Leslie Caron, Wilma Rudolph, Judy Garland, Aime Cesaire, Herman Hesse, The Artist Formerly Known As Prince, Meryl Streep, Shirley Bassey, Kevin Costner, Clark Gable, William Holden, Vanessa Redgrave, Dollie Parton, Jackie Robinson, Vincent Van Gogh, Mariah Carey, John Major, Eddie Murphy, Michaelangelo, John Denver, James Baldwin, Harrison Ford, Jerry Garcia, Mary Ford, Woody Allen, Maria Callas, Charles De Gaulle, Alfred Hitchcock, Werner Erhard, Julius Erving, Ted Kennedy, Kathie Lee Gifford, Lou Rawls, Elizabeth Taylor, Pete Sampras, Indira Gandhi, Yves Montand, Mike Ditka, Ted Roosevelt, Norah Jones, Jennifer Lopez, Dame Tanni Grey-Thompson, Lawrence Harvey.

Fidel Castro   2/2   8CWF
George Chambers former Trinidad and Tobago PM 9/7   8CWF
Frank Worrell Cricketer 4/3   8CWF
Jit Samaroo steelband arranger   2/2   8CWF
Anthony Williams steelband arranger   6/1   8CWF
Sami Hyypiä   Finnish football manager 9/7   8CWF
Wintley Phipps Vocal artist 1/6 8CWF
Oscar Niemeyer Brazilian architect, 3/4 8CWF
Sir Shridath "Sonny" Ramphal 9/7   8CWF
Alenka Bratusek   Slovenia politician 3/4 8CWF
Cesária Évora Cape Verde singer 2/2 8CWF
Denise Belfon Soca singer 2/2   8CWF
Roaring Lion Calypsonian 2/2   8CWF
Alison Hinds Soca singer 2/2   8CWF
Destra Garcia Soca singer 2/2 8CWF
Viv Richards West Indies cricketer 3/4   8 CWF
Clive Lloyd West Indies cricketer 2/2   8 CWF

7 Metal Contextual Winning Field

You will find your Contextual Winning Field incredibly receptive to your approaches if you use the following strategies:

1. Acceptance of life experiences and flexibility: let these principles guide you. The capacity to yield in challenging situations will develop deep inner strength, for to do so is a clear indication of being centred. Strive to cultivate this attitude.

2. Be aware of the virtue of give and take. Never take your blessings for granted. Always seek to give back to those who have been generous to you. Also express that attitude to nature, to the birds and animals. I suggest that you make offerings of food, water, flowers, candles or stone to this natural realm. This will open up new pathways for you to engage with life, pathways that can easily become closed down in the case of the number 7 Metal Contextual Winning Field personality. This closed quality could result in a scenario where you were attempting to engage life without all your cylinders firing.

3 Look after your lungs. Make time to breathe in the fresh air of the countryside, at the seashore or in the mountains at least for one day every ten days, especially if you live in a big city. Foods that support the lungs are rice, oats, sweet potatoes, ginger, lotus root, string beans, tempeh, mustard greens and spring onion. Marshmallow root and slippery elm also have great nutritional value for the lungs.

4. Lie on your back with a Japanese Zafu cushion under the arch of your lower back. This will create an opening up of your rib cage and solar plexus area. Allow yourself to breathe through your mouth with relaxed jaws. This exercise is liberating to any stuck emotions. Emotions of all types are always linked to your lungs, as immediately your emotions shift, your breathing changes. Your breath is the shadow of your emotions.

5. The colours white and cream will support your best efforts. Be cautious with red and pink, especially at peak times of creative expression. Your presentation should always carry elegance. However casually you may be dressed, keep that dash of exquisiteness in your clothes and bearing. Pay particular attention to the texture of clothing next to your skin, and especially around your throat. Choose these materials for their sensory qualities of touch, and allow this to nourish your being.

6. Massage some eucalyptus oil on the 3rd joint of your ring fingers, the joint closest to your palm. Massage it for at least 60 seconds. This is a reflex region for your lungs. Then, lay on your zafu as in the exercise listed above. A new treat awaits you: you will feel as if you have a third lung.

7. Protect yourself from dry conditions. It is best to massage some Young Living essential oil of nutmeg on the inside of your nostrils and ears. Best for the nutmeg oil to be mixed 50/50 with cold pressed sesame oil. Foods that neutralize dry conditions such as sweet rice, quinoa, millet, well-cooked oats, hiziki, peaches and oranges will be most helpful when faced with such dry conditions.

8. Seek beauty, and have it around you. Have fragrant white flowers around you. Place them in an exquisite vase that brings a clear focus to your living space. Let harmonious background music embrace your working environment.

9. Develop a sensory awareness of your skin: make friends with the nerve endings under the skin, and be aware of how sweetly they carry clear messages and experiences to your brain. In the same way you see with your eyes, cultivate a "seeingness" with your skin. This will add to your creative expression and also develop subtler forms of communication with yourself and your environment. Following these strategies will strengthen your connection to your Contextual Winning Field.

FAMOUS 7 METAL CONTEXTUAL WINNING FIELD PERSONALITIES

Earl Mountbatten, Carly Simon, Michael Caine, Kriss Kristofferson, Gina Lollabridgida, Oscar Wilde, Chuck Berry, Michael Collins, Theolonius Monk, Pablo Picasso, Luciano Pavarotti, Naomi Campbell, Harold Robbins, Sir Lawrence Olivier, Bob Geldof, Jimmy Carter, Sting, Damon Hill, T.S. Eliot, Rachel Welch, Boris Becker, Sri Chinmoy, Richard Gere, Richard Pryor, Mikhail Gorbachev, Michael Jackson, Bruce Lee, Toni Morrison, Smokey Robinson, Richard Branson, Billy Eckstine, Jackie Onassis, O.J.Simpson, Dag Hammarskjold, Carlos Santana, Carl Jung, Count Basie, John Lennon, Dan Rather, David Ben Gurion, Julia Roberts, Marc Anthony, Vivien Leigh, Tommy Hearns, Martha Stewart.

Quintin O'Connor Trinidadian politician 2/3 7CWF

Marc Edmund Jones Astrologer/philosopher 4/1   7CWF

Mary McLeod Bethune 8/6 7CWF Educator, Civil Rights leader

Elias Canetti Bulgarian Nobel winner 8/6 7 CWF

Thich Nhat Hanh Buddhist teacher 2/3   7 CWF

Coleman Hawkins   Jazz saxophonist   6/8 7CWF

6 Metal Contextual Winning Field

You will find your Contextual Winning Field incredibly receptive to your approaches if you use the following strategies:

1. Be accountable in all that you do. A code of ethics and honouring a compassionate value system will support your peace of mind. Cultivate this need that is present in your life: forget about what the rest of the world is doing. When your inner dialogue operates with a clear conscience, a vast landscape of imaginative possibilities will open up for you.

2. Organize your time, organize your space, create clear structures in your life and set them up in a way that supports you rather than restricts you. Cultivate this as an attitude, rather than a chore or a "to do" item on your "To Do" list.

3. Look after your large intestine. Regular bowel movements are a must. Adjust your lifestyle and dietary habits if irregularities occur. Good eating habits to cultivate include the use of sea vegetables, flaxseed, fenugreek, parsnips, oats, broccoli and turnips in the daily diet. A few dried figs soaked in water and added to your menu daily is an excellent support for your large intestine.

4. The oriental practice of sitting in Seiza (i.e. your knee folded under your thighs) is very supportive to the large intestine. You can create some stimulation for the colon by breathing and rising up onto your toes for two seconds, then breathing out, extending your toes as you return to the Seiza position. Do a round of 18 repetitions.
5. The colours white and cream will support your best efforts. Be cautious with red and pink, especially at peak times of creative expression.

6. Massage the sides of your nostrils with a few drops of Young Living essential oil of pine mixed with sesame oil. Take your time to massage it in. Give yourself at least two minutes to do this. It is a great tonic for the sinuses, colon and brain activity.

7. Protect yourself from dry conditions. It is best to massage some nutmeg* oil on the inside of your nostrils and ears. Foods that neutralize dry conditions such as sweet rice, quinoa, millet, well-cooked oats, hiziki, peaches and oranges will be most helpful when faced with such weather.

8. Let your space be graced by simplicity and a Zen touch. Minimalism is your style. Choose quality in your purchases. Go for the finest, especially with your purchases of technological items. It is important that the textures of clothing and fabrics feel just right in your environment.

Following these strategies will strengthen your connection to your Contextual Winning Field.

FAMOUS 6 METAL CONTEXTUAL WINNING FIELD PERSONALITIES

Whitney Houston, Paul Volcker, Van Morrison, Althea Gibson, Brian Clough, Diana Ross, Tracy Austin, Robin Williams, Mick Jagger, Arthur Ashe, Wole Soyinka, Yoko Ono, Larry King, Jimi Hendrix, General Pinochet, Rudolf Steiner, Leo Tolstoy, Donny Hathaway, David Bowie, Colin Powell, Arthur C. Clarke, Al Green, Farah Fawcett, Albert Schweitzer, Barack Obama.

Tori Amos   Singer/songwriter   1/2   6CWF

Jay Z   Singer/songwriter 4/8   6 CWF

Beyonce   Singer/songwriter 1/2   6 CWF

General Sir Mike Jackson   2/1 6CWF

Seymour Hersh   9/3 6CWF Investigative journo

Sajid Javid British politician 4/8   6CWF

Bernard Hopkins Jr boxer   9/3   6CWF

Mayawati Kumari, Politican from Uttar Pradesh 9/3   6CWF

Christine Keeler 4/8   6 CWF

Jennifer Aniston   Actress 4/8   6 CWF

Kate Moss British model   9/3 6 CWF

Amy Winehouse British singer 8/4   6CWF

Alfred Adler   Psychologist   4/8   6

Giorgio Armani   3/9   6   Designer

Roberto Assagioli founder of Psychosynthesis 4/8   6

Maurice Bejart   2/1   6   ballet dancer

Robert Redford   1/2   6

Igor Stravinsky   Composer   1/4   7

Gloria Vanderbilt Actress, heiress, socialite   4/8   6

Booker T. Washington African American educator, author 9/3   6

H.G. Wells   Author   8/4   6

Ludwig Erhard   former German chancellor   4/8 6CWF

Kemal Atatürk founder of modern Turkey 2/1 6WS

Haile Gebre Selassie Ethiopian athlete   9/3 6CWF

Capt. Cipriani T&T politician 9/3   6CWF

Mighty Spoiler Calypsonian 2/1   6CWF

Anthony Carmona President of T&T   2/1   6CWF

Ellis Clarke former T&T president   2/1   6CWF

A.N.R Robinson former T&T president 2/1   6CWF

Eric Williams former Prime Minister of T&T   8/4   6

Dario Fo playwright   2/1   6

Federico Fellini   film director   9/3   6

Anna Magnani actress   2/1   6

Mogol   lyricist   1/2   6

Maria Sánchez Vicario   Tennis player 2/1 6

Ann Jones   Tennis player 8/4   6

Serena Williams   Tennis player   1/1   6

Budge Patty   Tennis player 4/8   6

Ashley Cooper Tennis player   1/1   6

Roger Federer Tennis player 1/2 6

Christina María Aguilera 2/1 6 CWF

5 Earth Contextual Winning Field

You will find your Contextual Winning Field incredibly receptive to your approaches if you use the following strategies:

1. Let balance be the ongoing source of guidance in all that you do. Otherwise you may gain notoriety for taking yourself into extreme positions, but you will pay a price with poor health and self-destructive behavior, which can at times even lead to a premature death.

2. Perseverance, with a tenacious commitment to your chosen career, will certainly pay off. Doubts may arise, because at times nothing seems to be on the horizon: however, with that persistent tenacious quality, breakthroughs will occur.
3. Regular meal times are a must for maintaining your blood sugar levels. M
ake sure that you have hearty meals which feature pumpkin, squash, carrots, onions, cabbage and parsnips on the menu many times a week. Be cautious with your intake of fruit juices, alcoholic beverages and sugary items: they sabotage stable blood sugar levels.

4. The Taoist practice of clicking the teeth 36 times followed by the massaging of the upper and lower gums with the tongue nine times in each direction, then rinsing the saliva in the mouth before swallowing it in three gulps, is a wonderful ritual for you to do before any major effort. It will give your mind and system a clear signal that excellence is being called forth.

5. The colours yellow and gold and their various shades will support your best efforts. Be cautious with green, especially during peak times of creative expression.

6. Massage the region just below your navel in a clockwise direction for 60 seconds. Two great oils for this region are nutmeg oil and clove oil. Either of these oils will both bring a warmth and energy that will be very supportive for your pancreas and give you a boost in the morning.

This boost will create a feeling of possibility rather than clouds of doubt, the negative mindset that so often haunts 5 Earth Contextual Winning personalities.

7. Humidity and dampness sabotage your best efforts. If you are working in these types of conditions it would be important for you to avoid dairy food, peanuts, bananas, deep fried foods, coffee, alcohol, sugary-sweet items and foods that create mucous and phlegm in the body. Excellent foods that help to mop up dampness are celery, kohlrabi, turnips, scallions, amaranth, corn, rye, aduki beans, pumpkins pumpkin seeds, pumpkin seed butter and sesame seeds. Sitting for long periods can contribute to stagnation, which lends itself to dampness. Brisk walks every three hours if you are stuck in front of a computer are a must for keeping your creative juices flowing. Lotus root tea cuts through mucous and damp in your system like a hot knife through butter.

8. Images invoking the energy of stability should be present in your living space: they will impart feelings of sanity, steadfastness and dependability. Avoid clutter: keep your space clear and every week, have a clearing-out session. Clutter creates stagnation, and this is a key factor in sabotaging the best intentions of the 5 Earth Contextual Winning Field personality.

Following these strategies will strengthen your connection to your Contextual Winning Field.

FAMOUS 5 EARTH CONTEXTUAL WINNING FIELD PERSONALITIES

Helen Hayes, Roger Moore, Eamon De Valera, Miles Davis, Ho Chi Minh, Tony Blair, Fred Astaire, Marilyn Monroe, Peter Sellers, B.B.King, Brigitte Bardot, George Gershwin, Janis Joplin, Billie Holiday, Barbara Streisand, Douglas Mac Arthur, Paul Newman, Edgar Cayce, Ava Gardner, Sharon Stone, Jennifer Capriati, Willy Brandt, Camilla Parker-Bowles, Cat Stevens, Shirley Williams, John Steinbeck, Ted Turner, Charles Dickens, Che Guevara, Donald Trump, Sylvester Stallone.

Karl Hudson-Phillips   Trinidadian lawyer 4/6 5CWF

Wilfredo Lam   Cuban painter 8/2   5CWF

Clive Bradley Steelband arranger 1/9   5CWF

"Tim" Berners-Lee founder of the Web 9/1   5CWF

Steven Gerrard footballer   2/8 5CWF

Reverend Ike American prosperity preacher   2/8 5 CWF

Dane Rudhyar   Astrologer/Philosopher   6/4   5CWF

Kevin Durant basketball player 3/7   5CWF

Jose Marti Cuban poet 4/6   5CWF

Machel Montano Calypsonian   8/2   5CWF

David Rudder Calypsonian 2/8 5CWF

Rudranath Capildeo Mathematician/politician 8/2   5CWF

4 Wood Contextual Winning Field

You will find your Contextual Winning Field incredibly receptive to your approaches if you use the following strategies:

1. Let communication be your signature in life: this can include the written word, the spoken word, playing music, writing music or writing songs. Let this be the foundation that supports your life's efforts.

2. Persist with fortitude at creating your insights and value systems. Your style and approach with examples from your own life will inspire and touch many people. Through your commitment to communicate, breakthroughs of quantum proportions will occur in your life. Allow yourself to connect with that tenacious quality of being a messenger with what you do. At times, say nothing and keep silence until the rhythms of time have matured your perceptions. Patience with concerted efforts is a good standard to adopt in your life.

3. Look after your gall bladder. Limit your intake of fatty foods, especially in the evening: also, limit your intake of alcohol, mustard, eggs and spicy foods. Your gall bladder will feel the benefits of following a vegetarian diet. Having your last meal before 7 pm will also bring a glow to your gall bladder energy. It is beneficial to drink light, fragrant flower teas. Besides having unrefined grains on your menu, do include parsnips, sea vegetables, radishes, pears, lemons, mung beans, flax seeds and chamomile tea. Chewing some fennel seeds after a meal will be supportive to the functioning of your gall bladder.

4 Move your hips, rotating them in large circles to the left and to the right. Squat down so that you let go of your hips and buttocks as you relax your jaw and breathe through your mouth. The process of letting go and allowing will always serve your creative process. The Japanese corrective Sotai exercises are truly phenomenal in supporting 4 Contextual Winning Field personalities. I have seen this time and again in my practice with clients. Sotai creates this deep, spacious quality in the mind so that more time seems to be available to these personalities.

The "crush of time" that plagues 4 Contextual Winning Field people, where they always seem to be playing catch-up with their engagement diary, appears to diminish when they have these Sotai exercises as a daily practice. Yoga is also of great benefit: it is just that much more time would be needed with yoga to get the results that Sotai brings.

5. The colours turquoise and light blue and blue-green hues and shades will support your best efforts. Be cautious with white, especially in peak times of creative expression. Please be aware that if your chosen profession is one that requires you to wear white, an antagonistic colour for 3 and 4 Wood Contextual Winning Fields, you would be better off changing jobs unless that work is your true passion. If it IS your true passion, you need to find some way to balance things: for example, a small green item somewhere on your clothing. In addition, a fierce single-mindedness will give you the winning edge.

6. Relax your jaws when tension and stress builds. Massage your jaws, get your fingers stuck into the muscles that are in front of your ears and work along the jaw line in small circular movements.

7. Protect yourself from windy conditions. Wear a scarf. If you have to work in a windy or draughty environment for extended periods, it is best to massage some nutmeg* oil on the inside of your nostrils and ears. Hold a few fennel seeds with a bit of rosemary in your mouth as you go into the wind. At times, going into the wind can create major breakthroughs for 4 Contextual Winning Field personalities, and periods of indecisiveness can be resolved.

8. Chant, sing, whistle, practice public speaking. Engage your voice and its many attributes. Get it exploring certain ranges of expression. This will allow a greater sense of freedom in your self-expression. You can take this even further by massaging a drop of sandalwood essential oil in a small area on both sides of cervical vertebra 4. Now, shift your attention to a small area each side of the centre of your Adam's Apple: a drop of sandalwood essential oil gently massaged here will add to a greater range of expression with your voice.

9. A quote, a piece of poetry, lyrics from a song: whatever enrolls you to step forward with enthusiasm in life... place it prominently at a focal spot in your living space. Let it be well lit, so that it can be easily observed. Read it aloud from time to time as you enter the room.

10. Always be ready to write your dreams down, as some times prophetic and life changing dreams do arise: it will be very supportive to have a record of these. Following these strategies will strengthen your connection to your Contextual Winning Field.

FAMOUS 4 WOOD CONTEXTUAL WINNING FIELD PERSONALITIES

Eric Clapton, Anwar Sadat, Tony Williams, Hans D. Genscher, Ernest Hemingway, Salvador Allende, Salvador Dali, D.H. Lawrence, F. Scott Fitzgerald, Kofi Annan, Ravi Shankar, Audrey Hepburn, Glen Campbell, Jerry Brown, Bill Clinton, Robert Redford, Keanu Reeves, Mother Teresa, George B. Shaw, Bill Cosby, Stanley Kubrick, Linda Ronstadt, Brad Pitt, Monica Lewinsky.

Raul Castro 6/2   4CWF

Sonny Ramadhin West Indies cricketer 8/9   4CWF

Patrick Manning former Trinidad and Tobago PM 9/8   4CWF

Mighty Terror Calypsonian 8/9 4CWF

Mighty Sparrow   Calypsonian 2/6 4CWF

Cheddl Jagan Guyanese father of the nation 1/7 4CWF

Priyanka Chopra Indian politician 9/9 4CWF

"Jim" Rohn Motivational speaker 7/1   4CWF

Dame Iris Murdoch Novelist/Philosopher 9/9 4CWF

Mamata Banerjee Indian politician 1/7 4CWF

Banerjee is a self-taught painter and a poet

Russell Simmons 7/1 4CWF Founder of Def Jam label

3 Wood Contextual Winning Field

You will find your Contextual Winning Field incredibly receptive to your approaches if you use the following strategies:

1. Seek enthusiasm: let it be like Manna from Heaven. This is the key to creating breakthroughs in your life. Always find ways to have enthusiasm pumping you up with what you do.

2. Be prepared to create, paint, write, design, or play in any circumstance. Your creative juices can switch on at any time, especially if you are fully focused and committed with your projects. Have that pen and paper handy, have that game in your car: whatever is needed, have easy access to it. That bolt of creative lightning can hit you at any time. Give yourself permission to break your routines so that you can pursue your hunches.

3. Look after your liver. Include a folic acid supplement, best taken as the highlight in a B-complex vitamin formula. Start your day with the freshly squeezed juice of half a lemon in a cup of hot water. Let your menu include amaranth, quinoa, rye, mung beans, millet, watercress, celery and asparagus. Include the following spices: turmeric, basil, fennel, rosemary and the various mints.

4. Make it physical! Stretch your muscles, allow them to reach out, allow them to surrender to gravity so that new ways of expression can come forth. In that spacious mind that arises when you allow your muscles to surrender to gravity, it is possible to have glimpses of wisdom arise from your perceptions. On the other hand, to put some grit behind your muscles so that they are pushing against resistance will have another kind of impact on your mental state. This will be like squeezing out the finest drops of the elixir from the pips. In this way, cultivate your physical activity.

6. Embrace the colour green and its many shades, tones and hues in your wardrobe and in your living space. Please be aware that if your chosen profession is one that requires you to wear white, an antagonistic colour for 3 and 4 Wood Contextual

Winning Fields, you would be better off changing jobs unless that work is your true passion. If it IS your true passion, you need to find some way to balance things: for example, a small green item somewhere on your clothing. In addition, a fierce single-mindedness will give you the winning edge. Observe the qualities that brought Bjorn Borg and Steffi Graf to their Wimbledon titles and you will find this trait very present.

7. Marma point KURPARA at the back of your right elbow is massaged with JUVA CLEANSE. This is the best blend of oils for your liver. Shake the bottle vigorously then rub it between your hands a few times, slowly open it and with your feet flat on the ground take a smooth gentle smell of this blend of oils. Gently breathe it in from the soles of your feet a few times. Then put some on your left middle finger and massage it into the bone just above the back of your right elbow. If it does feel tight, do gently persevere with the massage of this oil into the marma point KURPARA: this will create an openness within your mind and body.

8. Protect yourself from windy conditions. Wear a scarf. If you have to work in such an environment for extended periods, it is best to massage some nutmeg oil on the inside of your nostrils and ears. Massaging the soles of your feet at night before going to sleep can also be helpful in supporting you in windy conditions.

9. Let your living space be one that startles you at the same time that it inspires you. There should be a feeling about being lifted up as you enter this space, you should feel energized and stimulated.

Following these strategies will strengthen your connection to your Contextual Winning Field.

FAMOUS 3 WOOD CONTEXTUAL WINNING FIELD PERSONALITIES

Buckminster Fuller, Mahatma Gandhi, Rabindranath Tagore, Curtis Mayfield, John Coltrane, Greta Garbo, Wayne Shorter, Lawrence of Arabia, Orde Wingate, Doris Lessing, Bill Gates, General George Patton, Steffi Graf, Will Smith, Michael Douglas, Julie Andrews, Charlton Heston, David Blunkett, Agatha Christie, Kobe Bryant, Paul McCartney, Freddie Laker, Pablo Neruda, Pierre Trudeau, Bjorn Borg, Segolene Royal, Gordon Ramsey, Manmohan Singh.

Molly Ahye Trinidadian choreographer 4/2 3CWF

Basdeo Panday Former PM of Trinidad & Tobago 4/2   3

Mighty Shadow Calypsonian 2/4   3CWF

Black Stalin   Calypsonian   2/4   3CWF

Norman Manley Former Jamaican PM 8/7   3CWF

Deepak Chopra New Age guru   9/6   3 CWF

Dinah Washington Jazz singer 4/2 3 CWF

Jakushitsu Genkō Zen Master 8/7 3CWF

Kate" Bush   6/9   3CWF

Shami Chakrabarti[British lawyer 4/4   3CWF

Jayalalithaa Jayaram 7/8   3CWF Indian Actress, politician

Josephine Baker Dancer/entertainer 4/2 3CWF

2 Earth Contextual Winning Field

You will find your Contextual Winning Field incredibly receptive to your approaches if you use the following strategies:

1. Put your head down and persist. Persistency, dedication and consistency will get results.

2. It is best to have a team that is part of your support base in bringing out your finest creative efforts. This team can be as basic as a few people who are confidantes with whom you share and discuss your projects. Team building activities definitely serve your creative efforts.

3. Look after your stomach. Make time for enjoying your meals. Bring feelings of gratitude to the table as you sit and enjoy the experience of chewing your food well. Warm and hot beverages will create a harmonious stomach.

4. Resting your palms over the left side of your rib cage and keeping them there until the gurgling sound releases your midriff energy centres is a good tonic for integrating mind and body. This ritual will develop a deeper communication with your nervous system, and prime it to provide full support in ventures and projects where you need it.
5 Orange is your colour. Wear it and bring it into your environment in the form of pens, scarves, hats etc. It is best to avoid green.

6. Massage the inside of the base of your left thumb: you will find a nodule. Massage it gently but firmly between your right thumb and forefinger. This stimulates the functioning of the stomach.

7. Humidity and dampness sabotage your best efforts. Excellent foods that remove dampness are celery, kohlrabi, turnip, scallion, amaranth, corn, rye, aduki beans, pumpkin, pumpkin seeds, pumpkin seed butter, sesame seeds. Limit your intake of dairy food, peanuts, bananas, deep fried foods, coffee, alcohol, sugary-sweet items

and foods that create mucous and phlegm in the body if you are working in humid or damp conditions. Sitting for long periods can contribute to stagnation, which lends itself to dampness. Brisk walks every three hours if you are stuck in front of a computer is a great tonic to keep your creative juices flowing, as is bouncing on a rebounder.

8. An atmosphere of warmth and sociability in your living space will create a sense of bonding for the 2 Earth Contextual Winning Field personality. Team spirit is immediately felt when such a room is entered.

9. "NOW!" and how you deal with the Present Moment requires a caring quality. You need to "look after" Time, and perceive it as a living being. When this takes place, you will feel less threatened by Time and "Now!"

An interesting thing starts to happen when you do this: you start to realize that Time is, indeed, on your side. Time more or less says "I have to protect you and look after you now."

It would seem that Nelson Mandela at some level adopted this response to Time during his 27 years in prison. Mandela is a 2 Earth Contextual Winning Field personality.

Following these strategies will strengthen your connection to your Contextual Winning Field.

FAMOUS 2 EARTH CONTEXTUAL WINNING FIELD PERSONALITIES

Harry Truman, Brooke Shields, Yasser Arafat, Isadora Duncan, Ronnie Biggs, Kenny G, Nelson Mandela, Princess Diana, Yves St Laurent, Wesley Snipes, Carl Lewis, Helen Keller, Lee Iacocca, Bruce Springsteen, Desmond Tutu, Nat King Cole, Cary Grant, Jane Fonda.

Beryl Mc Burnie Trinidadian choreographer 4/9 2CWF

Wyclef Jean   Haitian singer 4/9 2CWF

V.S. Naipaul Nobel prize winner 8/8   2CWF

Alf Valentine West Indies cricketer 7/6 2CWF

Garfield Sobers West Indies cricketer   1/3 2CWF

Jackie Wilson   R&B singer 3/1 2 CWF

Prabowo Subianto 4/9 2 CWF Indonesian politician

Joko Widodo 3/1   2 CWF Indonesian politician

Toni Michele Braxton   R&B singer   6/7 2CWF

James Packer Australian magnate   6/7 2CWF

Sebastian Kneipp Holistic health guru 8/8 2CWF

Bob Crow, trade unionist 3/1   2CWF

Caitlin Moran   7/6   2CWF Media personality

Johann Grander Water researcher/inventor 7/6 2CWF

Bill "Bojangles" Robinson Dancer/actor 8/8 2CWF

Tatiana Maslany actress 6/7 2CWF

Faith Hill   Country and Western singer 6/7 2CWF

1 Water Contextual Winning Field

You will find your Contextual Winning Field incredibly receptive to your approaches if you use the following strategies:

1. Create time for solitude, meditation or prayer. Connecting with that dimension called God, Nature or Emptiness will facilitate major breakthroughs in your life. Quiet walks by rivers, lakes or coastlines will also support you. Things will suddenly light up for you and fall into place.

2. Listen, listen, and listen. Pause from time to time and just listen. When in conversations, truly listen. Cultivating the activities of this sensory system will open more doors in your self-expression.

3. Look after your kidneys. They are the organs directly connected with your 1 Water Contextual Winning Field. Foods like aduki beans, black beans, buckwheat, root vegetables, warming vegetable soups and stews are recommended.

4. Regular walks will benefit the kidneys. Meditation does the same, as do any of the internal martial arts and Chi Kung.

5. Black and midnight blue are your colours: wear them, use them, have them around you. Be cautious with the colours yellow, orange and gold: they are antagonistic to your Contextual Winning Field.

6. Massage your ears. Cross your arms in front of your chest and have your right hand massage your left ear and your left hand massage your right ear. Give the ears a good rub for at least a minute. Then cover your right ear with the palm of your left hand and tap the back of your left hand with the fingers of your right hand. Do this for about 20-30 seconds and repeat on the left ear.

7. Keep yourself warm, avoid draughts. If the weather is windy, do keep a scarf around your neck. When the weather gets cold, it is wise to wear a hat or cap. In the winter keep your lower back warm.

8. Feeling comfortable in your inner space will allow you to be more aware and receptive to what is happening around you. This invites a mood of self-reflection. A sense of spaciousness and a deeper internal openness arises. Enjoy this feeling.

9. Quality sleep is a must to ensure optimal performance. Discover what pattern of sleep works for you. Do you feel better when you go to bed early and wake early? Or are you someone who loves the intensity of working late into the night and then surrendering to the embrace of your bed as sleep and its magical balm restores you? Make sure that you go to bed consciously, rather than fully clothed and drifting off in a stupor of tiredness. Maybe have a shower before going to bed as you prepare yourself to surrender to sleep. Let your bedroom be tidy, with pleasant fragrances.

10. Record your dreams. It is good to have access to more of this dimension in your life. Writing your dreams down as they occur will open you to more of this subconscious guidance.

11. Darkness and stillness can create a lot of clarity and insights for you. Your brain receptors and the nervous system become more open when you make time for such experiences.

Following these strategies will strengthen your connection to your Contextual Winning Field.

FAMOUS 1 WATER CONTEXTUAL WINNING FIELD PERSONALITIES

U Thant, James Joyce, Muhammad Ali, Duke Ellington, Hugh Hefner, Oprah Winfrey, W.A. Mozart, Winston Churchill, Gen. Franco, Walt Disney, Handel, Calvin Klein, Eva Peron, Monica Seles, Sigmund Freud.

Leroy Clarke Trinidad artist 8/3 1CWF

Kamla Persad-Bissessar P.M. of Trinidad & Tobago   3/3   1CWF

Solomon Hochoy Former Governor General of TT 2/9 1CWF

Prof. Arthur Lewis Nobel Prize winner 2/9   1CWF

Michael Manley   Former Jamaican P.M. 4/7   1CWF

Robert Greenidge West Indies cricketer   2/9   1CWF

Max" Keiser TV personality 2/9   1CWF

Viktor Schauberger   Water researcher 7/4 1CWF

 Max" Clifford   British PR guru   3/3   1CWF

Rev. Run   Precher/rapper   9/2 1CWF

Lloyd Best Trinidadian Economic professor 3/8   1CWF

Clyde Walcott West Indies cricketer 3/3   1CWF

Everton Weekes West Indies cricketer 3/8   1CWF

Uriah Butler Trinidadian politician   2/9 1CWF

CHAPTER 4

Your contextual winning time: what to do & what to avoid

My favourite things in life

don't cost any money.

It is really clear

that the most

precious resource

we all have is time.

Steve Jobs

CHAPTER 4
Your contextual winning time: what to do & what to avoid

You always have a choice. This is a time of high energy, energy that needs to have a focus and a plan, with clear goals as to what you want to achieve.

If you DON'T have this kind of focus, and simply sit there waiting for life to show you which direction to go, you will create a number of high-stress experiences that can easily manifest as health challenges and/or idiotic decisions that cost you plenty in terms of time, money and energy.

In this Chapter, you will first be given very clear guidelines as what TO DO: you will also be given suggestions about what NOT to do during your Contextual Winning Time.

GENERAL GUIDELINES

1. Cultivate the habit of wearing your contextual winning colour, and let that be around you, including things like the colour of your pen, your scarves, your ties etc. Invite this energy into your life.

2. Let your work projects receive quality time. As you keep focusing and working on these dreams that you wish to materialise, you will receive new insights, angles and qualities of contextual winning and a deeper creativity will shine through.

3. Make time for brain integration exercises. One not-so-obvious approach is to create "happy hours" for your brain. This quality of lightness is important. Let smiles and laughter come from you as you make time for juggling, playing with coloured pens, etc. Always look to juxtapose contrasting colours as you play with the pens and with

your creations. Be ridiculous, and let the playful child be present. Get on the merry-go-round or swings in a play park, and play. These activities stimulate your vestibular system, that part of the nervous system that takes your sensory experiences into your brain. The more integrated this system is, the more enhanced your brain functions will be.

4. Drink water, plain water, and lots of it. Dehydration is the secret saboteur of some of the best-laid creative efforts. Drinking plenty of water facilitates an easier flow in your creative process.

5. Be flexible about the physical positions you adopt in order to make breakthroughs. When you feel stuck, change position. Stand on the chair with a pencil and read the same paragraphs that are not working for you. If you are creating music, listen to the music while standing on the chair. If you are painting, look at the painting from under the table or lie on the floor and get a fresh position to approach things that are not coming together for you.

6. Have music in your environment. Yes, play those Bach and Mozart pieces: it has long been established that the music of these composers' supports integrated brain functioning. You will also have music that shakes you and moves you and leaves you inspired and uplifted. Play those pieces. This is your time to stretch yourself and make breakthroughs. GO FOR IT! Let music be a support in taking you there.

7. Play with fragrances. Have them present in the room in which you work and create. Personally, I love the Young Living Essential Oils: I diffuse them all the time. One of my favourite blends is CITRUS FRESH. I find this immediately lifts the spirits. One that makes a big difference is BRAIN POWER, especially when I have deadlines with creative work. A truly magical one is EXODUS II: This blend seems to create space and ease in working with what's in front of you. Explore, investigate, discover for yourself what works for YOU with fragrances.

8. Practice eye exercises daily, especially if you spend a lot of time in front of a computer. Keeping these "tools of vision" well oiled and maintained will bring ease and an enthusiasm to get on with your projects. Plus, you will find that your mood

will be more pleasant and light. The liver governs the eyes and when you create joy for the eyes, you lower frustration levels and impatience. Excellent qualities to have in ready supplies during your Contextual Winning Field time. (See eye exercises listed below this chapter.)

9. Change your habitual patterns of doing routine actions during the first hour after waking. Do at least one thing differently, but no more than two. For example, if you normally scrub your teeth with your toothbrush in you left hand, use your right hand. If you brush your hair with the brush in your right hand, have it in your left hand instead. If you always put your right slipper on first, put your left one on first instead. This approach will wake the brain up and create a curiosity and sharpness in your responses to life, and you will find that the qualities of your Contextual Winning Field will unfold more bountifully.

10 Ensure that your nutritional needs are well met. In addition to looking after the obvious things, such as adequate intake of vitamins, minerals and amino acids from your food and supplements, you also need to look at your essential fatty acid intake. These fatty acids are crucial for optimal brain functioning.

Here is the specific "To Do" list for each Contextual Winning Field:

NINE FIRE CONTEXTUAL WINNING FIELD

1. Bring it on to the front burner

2. Cultivate a mood of calmness

3. Exercise so that you break into a sweat

4. Practice yogic "fire breathing"

5. Massage your scalp

EIGHT EARTH CONTEXTUAL WINNING FIELD

1. Make time for voluntary work for those less fortunate than yourself.

2. Demonstrate your resourcefulness by putting food out for the birds.

3. Persevere with your goals, regardless of the challenges.

4. Massage your navel with a little warm nutmeg oil thirty six times in a clockwise direction.

5. Dip a hand towel in hot water, squeeze out the excess, and use the towel to vigorously brush your skin.

SEVEN METAL CONTEXTUAL WINNING FIELD

1. Cultivate an elegance of expression to inform all your actions.

2. Choose white and cream as the colours for your clothes and environment.

3. Keep a small, beautiful object in your pocket that inspires you through the sense of touch.

4. Breathe in deeply for a count of 6, hold for a count of 6 and breathe out slowly for a count of 12. This is all done with ease and smoothness. Engage with this practice any time the impulse occurs to slip into anxiety and worry.

5. Warm two white stones by squeezing them in your hands. Lie on you back, and place a stone in the slight indentation at the front of each shoulder, a little below the clavicle. Cross the arms over the chest, and place one palm over each stone. Rest in this position for five minutes. Give yourself permission to feel what arises as you close your eyes whilst doing this.

SIX METAL CONTEXTUAL WINNING FIELD

1. Seek to cultivate a devotional heart.

2. Have your bedroom be minimalist in its content and presentation: let white be the dominant colour.

3. Put aside the final thirty minutes before sleep to be a time when you seek to complete your day with a peaceful mind.

4. Cultivate a ritual of tidying up your desk when you finish work for the day.

5. Develop the habit of regularly reading a few Haiku poems from the Japanese poets Basho, Issa, Buson or Shiki.

FIVE EARTH CONTEXTUAL WINNING FIELD

1. Maintain a deep sense of faith as you visualize achieving your goals.

2. Cultivate feelings of full confidence with your self-expression.

3. Stand up and do some stretching movements for five minutes every hour.

4. Maintain your blood sugar levels by eating regular meals.

5. Chew a few cardamom seeds from time to time during the day.

FOUR WOOD CONTEXTUAL WINNING FIELD

1. Respond promptly to all forms of communication.

2. Keep a daily journal.

3. Seek to resolve conflicts promptly through dialogue: cultivate a soft voice for doing this.

4. Drink some saffron water in the mornings a few times a week on an empty stomach.

5. Explore the practice of Sotai.

THREE WOOD CONTEXTUAL WINNING FIELD

1. Be open to flashes of inspiration while maintaining your blood sugar levels.

2. Keep a regime of daily physical activity for at least half an hour.

3. Cultivate flexibility as a guiding principle as you approach challenges.

4. Take time to relax your muscles. Cultivate a habit of deliberately letting go from head to toe. Do ten-minute bouts of this exercise a few times every day.

5. Walk in the woods. If this is not possible, try to spend a few minutes gazing into a wood or forest.

TWO EARTH CONTEXTUAL WINNING FIELD

1. Practice being a good host or hostess.

2. Seek a mentor, and learn from them.

3. Make time to cultivate friendships.

4. Click your teeth together thirty six times and move your tongue back and forth along your front teeth nine times. Slowly swallow the saliva generated in this way, visualizing it as orange nectar soothing your stomach.

5. Whilst standing, bring your bent left leg up behind you with your left hand, and give it a good stretch as you breathe out. Repeat the exercise with your right leg.

ONE WATER CONTEXTUAL WINNING FIELD

1. Be willing to go the extra mile.

2. Get a good night's sleep. This is your best tonic.

3. Be receptive to guidance from your dreams.

4. Rub your lower back in a circular motion with the back of your wrists thirty six times.

5. Always ensure that your lower back is kept warm.

WHAT TO AVOID DURING YOUR CONTEXTUAL WINNING FIELD TIME

It is important to realise that the time of your Contextual Winning Field is a time of high energy, even sometimes of great intensity. It is therefore important to be clear and precise about your actions rather than operating from hope with what you are doing. Clear focus, articulated end results and a very present sense of tangibility about what you are doing are some obvious factors required for any important undertaking during these periods. Here is a simple "avoid" list.

1. Avoid rash decisions and "hoping for the best". Such actions will bring added stress to your situation, more so than at other times.

2. Avoid irregular eating habits. Now is the time to have your meal times organised and focused. Time spent doing this will pay major dividends in heightened creativity.

3. Avoid alcohol and sweet-tooth binges. The pancreas is the organ involved, regardless of your Contextual Winning Field during this period. Maintaining stable blood sugar levels is an important factor in supporting peak performance at this time.

4. Avoid taking on new projects where you have no expertise or experience: it would just create frustration.

5. Avoid ignoring time management principles. It is important to have a game plan, with time put aside for accessing your heightened creative potential.

6. Avoid having routine matters dominate your time during this period. This is not the best time to have your teeth fixed, house painted, computer serviced, car repaired, and accounts done. Such activities will leave you very impatient and irritable during this period.

7. Avoid long distance travel, unless it is specifically part of a planned Contextual Winning Field project. Should this be the case, plan it carefully, ensuring that the travel is in an auspicious direction for that time. (See Chapter 13 of my book Grasshopping Through Time for guidance about this.)

8. Avoid impulsive choices and definitely do not make impulsive decisions at this time.

9. Avoid changing residence or offices. In a way, this is a time for stabilising yourself, for perceiving and connecting with new possibilities so that you can experience a quantum leap in your creativity. Sometimes, the quantum leap is about realising new approaches to your life, and other ways of doing things.

10 Avoid wearing colours that are antagonistic to your Contextual Winning Field colour during this period.

11. Avoid going against the core recommendations of your Contextual Winning Field

12. Avoid buying into people's comments about what you can and can't do. Persevere with the visions and dreams you have about your life. This period is a time when you can certainly actualise them, or at least move them forward many steps.

13. Avoid cramming your diary with social engagements. You will want to have more spacious time for yourself and to be with confidantes and/or loved ones who are at the heart of your creative efforts.

Do not dwell in the past,

do not dream of the future,

concentrate the mind

on the present moment.

Buddha

CHAPTER 5

How to use your contextual winning field for health, well-being & self-expression

When you are content
to be simply yourself
and don't compare
or compete,
everybody
will respect you.

Lao Tzu

CHAPTER 5
How to use your contextual winning field for health, well-being & self-expression

In this chapter, you will find out how to create and enjoy maximum health and well-being from tips given to you by your friend and mentor, your Contextual Winning Field.

I have outlined these strategies under two distinct headings: Inner Space and Tactical Approaches. Let's take a look at these areas now.

THE CONTEXTUAL WINNING FIELD AND INNER SPACE

In modern life, people suffer from a fixation about external things. They worry about how they look, their weight, how well-defined their 8-pack is etc. Within the domain of The CWF, the foundation of your core health arises from deep inside you.

Evidence of this can be seen in the yogic traditions of Pranayama and the Taoist internal energy practices of Tai Chi and Chi Gung, all of which nourish the inner space.

FILLING INNER SPACE WITH YOUR CONTEXTUAL WINNING FIELD

These techniques can be practiced "in the real world" or in your imagination.

NINE FIRE CONTEXTUAL WINNING FIELD

Feel the heat of the sun warming you all over. Feel the warmth slowly moving into your lower belly. Feel the warmth as logs burn in a fire place, bringing heat and comfort to your body and energizing you for action. With a strenuous effort, climb to the top of a steep hill. Visualize masses of red flags blowing on top of a high mountain. Imagine the glow of hot embers warming your lower belly, creating a deep radiant glow within.

EIGHT EARTH CONTEXTUAL WINNING FIELD

Stand firm on the top of a hill as you feel the amber-coloured earth energy rising into your navel. Standing on a rebounder, gently rock backwards and forwards from your heels to your toes as the vibrations of this rocking flow through your cellular system. Lie on the floor and shake your arms and legs vigorously for one minute. Rest for two minutes, and repeat. Rest again for two minutes, and repeat the shaking one more time. Before showering, scrub the entire body with a skin brush or loofah. Afterwards, use a few drops of essential oil of Orange in a diffuser, rubbed between the palms and inhaled, or internally. Visualize an amber mountain and ask it to support you feeling closer to your 8 Earth Contextual Winning Field.

SEVEN METAL CONTEXTUAL WINNING FIELD

Brush your skin then feel the glow as you breathe deeply. Be totally enveloped in a beautiful sunset as you stand at the edge of a beach feeling the gentle waves caressing your feet. Stand by a frozen lake in a snow-covered forest as the silence and the whiteness envelops your senses. Gaze into a still, calm lake. As you gaze into the lake, notice the reflection of the sky above you, with a few white clouds. The fragrance of fresh eucalyptus fills the room, creating a sense of more space and elegance in your life.

SIX METAL CONTEXTUAL WINNING FIELD

You allow yourself to become one with the lone, tough rock that stands in the Zen sand garden. A sense of accountability, clarity and presence arises. This is it! Lie on the floor on a thick white blanket and relax until nothing exists except you and the thick white blanket. Continue to relax until you become the thick white blanket. Gaze into the deep blue sky and feel its all-pervasive presence in your life. Polish a mahogany table until it shines so bright that you realize the shine comes from the depth of the wood.

Frost on the garden grass

Leaf flits across your window

Autumn is here

FIVE EARTH CONTEXTUAL WINNING FIELD

Slowly sip a delicious pumpkin soup. Squeeze the meaty area below base of your right thumb as you clench and open your right fist. Complete a crossword puzzle. Assess in great detail what is needed so that things flow smoothly tomorrow. Lay on your belly, arms at your side, chin on the floor and slowly lift your legs as you breathe out. Breathe in as you slowly lower your legs. Repeat 5 times.

FOUR WOOD CONTEXTUAL WINNING FIELD

Sing your favourite song. Gargle with some warm salt water. Keep a dream diary. Listen to Eric Clapton's "Tears in Heaven". Massage your jaws.

THREE WOOD CONTEXTUAL WINNING FIELD

Stretch, allowing your body to surrender to gravity as you do so. Allow a feeling of "letting go" to flow through your muscles from head to toe. Allow your enthusiasm for your new project to arise and fill your muscles.
Consciously cultivate talking in a soft voice. Feel yourself "switched on" by an electrical storm: you become inspired and activated to follow your dreams.

TWO EARTH CONTEXTUAL WINNING FIELD

Take two cups. Fill one cup with boiled hot water. Pour the hot water back and forth a few times between the cups. This will activate the water's Chi energy. You can now slowly sip the water. Sit and enjoy a delicious meal set on a linen tablecloth using quality glassware. Enjoy a cup of orange peel tea with your meal.
Chat openly with your confidante, enjoying laughter, warmth and closeness.
Place a bowl containing five oranges in your working area and break the skin of each one so that the fragrance of oranges fills the room. Have a warm, friendly conversation with your mother. If she has passed on, create a conversation in your imagination.

ONE WATER CONTEXTUAL WINNING FIELD

Soak in a hot bath to which has been added a cup of sea salt. Take a walk by a river, lake or sea where you can hear the sound of water. Sleep on dark blue sheets and pillow cases in your tidy, clutter-free bedroom. Massage your ankles and the soles of your feet with nutmeg oil. When taking a shower invite feelings of comfort from the water to cleanse and purify you. Sense the water as pure, deep light blessing you with contentment.

THE CONTEXTUAL WINNING FIELD AND TACTICAL APPROACHES

We begin this section with some examples from each Contextual Winning Field pattern of peak performers who have (albeit unconsciously) taken advantage of the magic of their Field to maximize their creative impact. For each Contextual Winning Field number these examples are followed, in red text, by four or five key tactical approaches that you can start using today to fine-tune your engagement with the world. Once again, examples of peak performers are given for each key tactical approach.

1 WATER CONTEXTUAL WINNING FIELD TACTICAL APPROACHES

3/8

Sammy Davis Jr

Sarah Vaughan

Omar Sharif

Queen Elizabeth II

Hugh Hefner

Oprah Winfrey

Ryan O'Neil

Jacques Villeneuve

Gen. Norman Schwarzkopf

Pandit Nehru

Imran Khan

George Harrison

Billie Jean King

Jack Lemmon

Bill Russell

Madame Chiang Kai-Shek

Duke Ellington

While some critics have understood Ellington's sense for religion to be expressed only in the three "Sacred Concerts" given near the end of his life, Janna Steed argues in her book "Duke Ellington, a Spiritual Biography" that Ellington always had an interest in spiritual matters, beginning at home and with church participation in Washington, DC.

His early compositions such as "Hymn of Sorrow" (1935) and "Come Sunday" (1943) evidence that interest. Steed cites Ellington's claim to be "a man of faith who regularly prayed and read his Bible."

She recounts that when a religiously-sensitive jazz singer objected to having vocal scatting and tap dancing in the First Sacred Concert, Ellington picked up the well-worn Bible in his dressing room and immediately found the passage in 2 Samuel from which he took the lyrics, "David danced before the Lord."

James Joyce

In "Ulysses", Joyce employs stream-of-consciousness, parody, jokes and virtually every other established literary technique to present his characters. The action of the novel takes place in a single day, 16 June 1904 (1 Water Month).

Each chapter employs its own literary style, and parodies a specific episode in Homer's "Odyssey". Furthermore, each chapter is associated with a specific colour, art or science and bodily organ. Joyce liked to wear a black hat and suit.

Gamal Nasser

A huge source of ideological inspiration to the Arab world

Franklin Delano Roosevelt

Had the conviction and determination to pursue his goals and aspirations in spite of setbacks. His complete paralysis from the waist down in 1921 (thought at the time to be the result of poliomyelitis, although a retrospective study in 2003 concluded that Roosevelt was suffering from Guillain–Barré syndrome) did not stop him pursuing his political career. Overcoming major social challenges, he came to power in the midst of the depression and the Nazi threat. Nevertheless, he inspired hope and belief in the common man.

Wolfgang Amadeus Mozart

Mozart has remained a source of inspiration to musicians around the world, including modern-day pop musicians and composers. Maurice White, the founder of the band Earth,Wind and Fire has acknowledged the inspiration that Mozart's music and compositions had on his own musical creations.

U Thant, 3rd Secretary-General of the United Nations

Thant was a devout Buddhist, a servant of peace who attempted to make things comfortable in difficult situations.

Dinah Shore

After failing singing auditions for the bands of Benny Goodman and both Jimmy Dorsey and his brother Tommy Dorsey, Shore struck out on her own to become the first singer of her era to achieve huge solo success.

She enjoyed a long string of over 80 charted popular hits, lasting from 1940 into the late 1950s, and after appearing in a handful of films went on to a four-decade career in American television, starring in her own music and variety shows in the 1950s and 1960s and hosting two talk shows in the 1970s.

Andre Agassi
Al Capone
Adolf Hitler
Angela Davis
Shirley MacLaine
Gregory Peck
Elvis Presley

Charlie Chaplin

Chaplin brought comedy, laughter and relief to the world while it was tearing itself apart during the First World War. Over the next 25 years, through the Great Depression and the rise of Hitler, he stayed on the job. It is doubtful whether any individual has ever given more entertainment, pleasure and joy to so many human beings when they needed it the most.

He played "The Tramp" dressed in black, and through the character's actions took a strong ideological position on social issues

Paul Robeson

Robeson maintained a persistent zeal through difficult and challenging times during the McCarthy years in1950s America.

Antonio Salazar Portuguese dictator, 1932-1968

Whatever one may think of his politics, Salazar was very successful in linking religious belief with political action.

4/7

Marlon Brando
Aretha Franklin
Frank Sinatra

Quincy Jones

Quincy Jones is an American music conductor, arranger, film composer, television producer and trumpeter. During 50 years in the entertainment industry, Jones has earned a record 79 Grammy Award nominations, 27 Grammys, and a Grammy Legend Award.

He is best known for his work with Frank Sinatra, Lesley Gore and his work with Michael Jackson as the producer of "Thriller", the biggest-selling album in music history, with current sales figures of 110 million. Jones allows things to flow into the world with his arrangements and music very much like an ocean with its currents.

Sarah Vaughan
Josef Stalin
Adolf Eichmann
Rush Limbaugh

7/4

Ezzard Charles
Ross Perot
Enoch Powell
Mike Tyson

8/3

Félix Houphouët-Boigny
Montgomery Clift
Dylan Thomas
Hillary Clinton
Dick Gregory
Chiang Kai Shek
Timothy Leary
Martina Navratilova
Eleanor Roosevelt

9/2

Candice Bergen
Cher
Winston Churchill
Francisco Franco
Tom Selleck
Josip Broz Tito
Roberta Flack

George Frideric Handel
Monica Seles
David Niven
Andy Williams
Jean Sibelius
Florence Nightingale
William Blake

Thomas Edison

Edison is the father of modern telecommunications. He founded General Electric, the largest publicly traded company.

Walt Disney

Disney played on our fascination with the imaginative feelings of childhood emotions when he hooked distinct names on to the animals in his movies. He founded Disney Inc., which has become the largest media and entertainment conglomerate in the world with an annual revenue of more than 37 billion dollars.

Sigmund Freud

Freud channelled his intense curiosity about the mind into deep explorations of the nature of human perception and the driving forces behind it.

1 WATER CONCEPTUAL WINNING FIELD PERSONALITIES

HAVE CONFIDENCE IN THE INTANGIBLE DIMENSION OF LIFE

Oprah Winfrey and her trust in a dimension beyond the physical realm.

Jean Sibelius and his total trust that musical inspiration would come to embrace him as he sat looking out over Lake Tuusula from his living room window.

Duke Ellington and his acknowledgement of the part that the Bible played in his life.

Sammy Davis Jr. turning to Judaism as he faced the biggest trials of his life.

William Blake's mystical attitude to life and his use of Biblical imagery in his poetry and paintings.

ARE IMAGINATIVE CREATORS

Sigmund Freud and his breakthrough theories about the human mind and the dimension of the unconscious.

Walt Disney and the creation of his animal personalities in animated film productions.

Sibelius' music, which arose from experiencing his symphonies first as colour impressions, before translating this into a musical score.

Winston Churchill and his consistent iconic use of the "V for Victory" sign, usually while wearing a black coat and a black hat. This image is the one he imprinted on the minds of the British public and The Allied Forces.

Hugh Hefner and the "Playboy Bunny" symbol with which he branded his Playboy empire.

Charlie Chaplin and his iconic "Tramp" character, always dressed in black suit, black hat, black umbrella and tie.

ARE SKILLFUL MASS COMMUNICATORS

Oprah Winfrey and her syndicated TV show, watched by millions globally.

Thomas Edison, the inventor of much of the technology underpinning modern communications systems.

Walt Disney productions, whose Mickey Mouse character is known by billions of people globally.

Elvis Presley as the personality that brought Rock and Roll to the world.

Charlie Chaplin film productions

Quincy Jones and his musical arrangements and production for the song "We are the World". Jones was the arranger for Michael Jackson's "Off The Wall" album, which sold more than 20 million copies and made Jones the most powerful record producer in the industry. He also produced "Thriller" for Jackson, an album which has to date sold more than 110 million copies and is the biggest-selling album of all time.

Quincy Jones also produced Jackson's album "Bad", which sold 32 million copies.

Hugh Hefner and his marketing of the Playboy business.

ARE PERSEVERING VISIONARIES

Gamal Nasser and the Pan Arabian ideology that he pursued even when confronted by British, French and Israeli forces after his seizure of the Suez Canal. He gave the order to the Egyptian Forces not to surrender.

Winston Churchill rallying the British people during World War II when they were being heavily bombed by the Nazis.

Marshal Josip Tito and the leadership qualities he demonstrated while leading the Yugoslavian freedom fighters against the Nazis during the second World War.

Franklin D. Roosevelt and his leadership of The United States through the Great Depression and World War II

Paul Robeson maintaining his Marxist revolutionary ideals even when stripped of his American passport and alienated and ostracized by mainstream black America.

Muhammad Ali persevering in his stand not to join the US Army on the grounds that he had no quarrels with the Viet Cong, for which he was stripped of the world heavyweight boxing title.

U Thant's attitude to the challenges he faced as Secretary General of the United Nations.

ENJOY SEEMINGLY EFFORTLESS ARTISTIC EXPRESSION

Duke Ellington's compositions and renditions were easy on the ear.

Mozart's work had an inherent harmonious structure that, according to many critics, takes his music closer to the Divine than any other classical composer.

Quincy Jones music and its global appeal.

Frank Sinatra's singing and the timing and phrasing in his songs.

George Harrison's composition "My Sweet Lord".

Elvis Presley's rock and roll music.
Roberta Flack and Sarah Vaughn's singing styles.

William Blake's paintings are filled with photographic accuracy in their depiction, and yet the feeling of familiarity from the deep Christian roots of the imagery is also apparent.

Handel's "Messiah" gives you the feeling to exclaim "Hallelujah!" at the appropriate moments.

2 EARTH CONCEPTUAL WNNING FIELD TACTICAL APPROACHES

1/3

Virginia Wade
Nelson Mandela
Yves St Laurent
Ingmar Bergman

3/1

Carl Lewis
Maradona
Helen Keller
Princess Diana
Patrice Lumumba

4/9

Leon Trotsky
Maradona
Eugene O'Neil
Leopold Senghor
Lee Iacocca

6/7

Brook Benton
Juan Peron

Lal Bahadur Shastri

Third Prime Minster of the Republic of India 1964-1966. While Shastri was a freedom fighter for Indian independence in the 1920s and 30s, he was imprisoned for a total of nine years by the British.

Once, while he was in prison, one of his daughters fell seriously ill. He was released for fifteen days, on the condition that he not take part in the freedom movement. However, his daughter died before he reached home. After performing the funeral rites, he voluntarily returned to prison, even before the expiration of agreed the period. A year later, he asked for permission to go home for a week, as his son had contracted influenza.

The permission was given, but his son's illness was not cured in a week. In spite of his family's pleadings, he kept his promise to the jail officers and returned to the prison.

Bruce Springsteen

Desmond Tutu

"His joy in our diversity and his spirit of forgiveness are as much part of his immeasurable contribution to our nation as his passion for justice and his solidarity with the poor."

Nelson Mandela, speaking at a thanksgiving for Tutu on his retirement as Archbishop in 1996

Barbara Walters

7/6
Sekou Toure
Boris Yeltsin
Emmanuel Swedenborg
George Forman
David Frost

Cary Grant
Linda Lovelace
Sugar Ray Robinson
Richard Nixon

8/8
Isadora Duncan
Sugar Ray Leonard
Bob Dylan
Yasser Arafat
Burt Bacharach
Johann Wolfgang von Goethe
Stevie Wonder
Harry Truman

Brooke Shields
Henry Kissinger
Toussaint L'Overture
Samuel Selvon

9/4

Maya Angelou
J.S.Bach
Warren Beatty
Jane Fonda
Liza Minnelli
Nat King Cole
Marlene Dietrich
Anthony Hopkins
Carlo Ponti
Rudyard Kipling

Patti Smith
Rock singer, political activist with a deep matriarchal response. "Because The Night" is one of her most popular songs with over five million views on YouTube (at May 15, 2014)

2 EARTH CONTEXTUAL WINNING FIELD PERSONALITIES

HAVE THE CAPACITY TO BE INSPIRED FROM THE SPIRITUAL DIMENSION

Emanuel Swedendborg's dream experiences and the guidance he received from other dimensions.

J. S. Bach also conceived the cruciform melody (among other similar ones) as a sign of devotion to Christ and the cross

Maya Angelou

Angelou has stated that she plays cards in order to get that place of enchantment, in order to access her memories more effectively. She has stated, "It may take an hour to get into it, but once I'm in it - ha! It's so delicious!" She does not find the process cathartic; rather, she has found relief in "telling the truth".

EXHIBIT A SINCERE CONCERN FOR HUMANITY

Nelson Mandela and the example of his life

Helen Keller and her ongoing efforts to help the downtrodden in society

Desmond Tutu and his outspoken stand for human rights and justice for all.

Bob Dylan's lyrics articulating a better tomorrow for all.

Emanuel Swedenborg's emphasis on charity and goodwill to the community.

Princess Diana's stand for Aids sufferers and for a ban on the military use of mines.

Lal Shastri's humility and sense of responsibility as a Minister and Prime Minister in Indian politics.

Bruce Springsteen's cultivating and endorsing his connection with New Jersey, his home state, and consistently expressing this connection even after becoming a global singer and entertainer.

Lee Iacocca's support for diabetics and for better health care and education for people suffering from this disease. He is also involved with an organization called "Nourish The Children" which has a global dimension to it.

ARE ICONIC IMAGE CREATORS

Marlene Dietrich's use of her body and voice to present the exotic feminine mystique that was her trademark persona as an actress and singer.

Yasser Arafat and his use of the keffiyeh, the Palestinian headscarf. Traditionally worn by Palestinian peasants, the keffiyeh became a symbol of Palestinian nationalism during the Arab Revolt of the 1930s. Its prominence increased in the 1960s with the beginning of the Palestinian resistance movement and its adoption by Arafat.

The keffiyeh would later become his trademark symbol, and he was rarely seen without a distinctively-arranged black-and-white scarf.

Isadora Duncan and the long flowing scarves that she loved to wear.

Ingmar Bergman and his style of crafting his films allowed many European women to come to terms with the sexual-emotional overtones in their lives.

Yves St Laurent fashion designs offered women another way of presenting themselves, with softer edges yet with an ease of function in modern life.

Princess Diana's persona and the things she spoke about enabled many people to acknowledge their emotional needs and shortcomings in a dignified way.

ENJOY THE CAPACITY TO OPENLY SHARE THEIR LIVES

Maya Angelou's open sharing of her childhood and the many experiences she has been through.

Brooke Shields and her sharing of her childhood experiences, loss of virginity and post-partum depression.

Emanuel Swedenborg's open sharing of his spiritual and psychic experiences, despite coming from a scientific and academic background, an environment that was very skeptical about such experiences.

Princess Diana and her open sharing about her challenges with eating disorders.

HAVE THE ABILITY TO RECREATE THEMSELVES

George Forman becoming a marketer of cooking devices. Apart from his advertisements for Meineke mufflers, Foreman also tours the world promoting the "George Foreman Lean Mean Fat Reducing Grilling Machine".Foreman has said that he has made more money from his grilling machine contracts than he made during his entire boxing career, and has suggested that he is better known for the grill than he is for his boxing. He also is a Christian preacher with his own parishioners.

Jane Fonda switching from a career as a highly successful movie actress, then becoming a keep fit guru and a political activist.

Bob Dylan's ongoing changes in his musical style which has included folk, rock and roll, blues, gospel. Dylan continues to reinvent himself as a musician.

Lee Iacocca has moved from CEO of Chrysler to a social advocate for national issues affecting American society.

ARE CULTURAL ICONS

Bob Dylan's music, song writing and attitude to the status quo has been a symbol of the American counter culture since the 60s.

Yasser Arafat has been an icon for Arabs and Palestinians.

Nelson Mandela has remained an icon for the South African liberation and has now almost become a brand name for anything that is ethical in the world.

Ingmar Bergman's movies and style represented a certain elegance and statement about sophistication for European movie-goers.

Leopold Senghor, the Senegalese poet and politician, was an icon for the Négritude movement, a literary and ideological movement developed by francophone black intellectuals, writers, and politicians in France in the 1930s who found solidarity in a common black identity as a rejection of French colonial racism.

They formed a realistic literary style and formulated their Marxist ideas as part of this movement, and acted as an inspiration and for black people everywhere, especially those coming out of the French colonial past seeking to embrace their African roots.

Marlene Dietrich was an icon on two fronts; as a German rallying against Nazi ideology and as an enigmatic woman with mystique.

3 WOOD CONTEXTUAL WINNING FIELD APPROACHES

2/4

George Jackson
Cannonball Adderley
Johnny Mathis
Jessie Jackson

Mahatma Gandhi
His loincloth and simple Indian dress was flamboyant at one level and yet was also a statement of his humility.

Greta Garbo
John Coltrane
Julie Andrews

Maya Ying Lin
is a Chinese-American artist and sculptor whose best known work is the Vietnam Veterans' Memorial in Washington D.C.

Han Suyin
Author of "A Many Splendored Thing", Medical doctor, novelist, lecturer

Jacqueline Bisset
English actress. "Her films include "Airport," "The Deep," and "Casino Royale."

4/2

Ingrid Bergman
Kobe Bryant
Joan Collins

Rabindranath Tagore
His long beard and princely demeanour created a striking presence when he entered a room.

Orson Welles
T.E. Lawrence
Wayne Shorter
James Baldwin

Maria Montessori
Aside from a new pedagogy, among the premier contributions to educational thought by Montessori are:

1. Instruction in 3-year age groups, corresponding to sensitive periods of development (for example: Birth-3, 3-6, 6-9, 9-12, 12-15 year olds with an Erdkinder (German for "Land Children") program for early teens.

2. Children as competent beings, encouraged to make maximal decisions.

3. Observation of the child in the prepared environment as the basis for ongoing curriculum development (presentation of subsequent exercises for skill development and information accumulation).

4. Small, child-sized furniture and creation of a small, child-sized environment (microcosm) in which each can be competent to produce overall a self-running small children's world.

5. Creation of a scale of sensitive periods of development, which provides a focus for class work that is appropriate and uniquely stimulating and motivating to the child (including sensitive periods for language development, sensorial experimentation and refinement, and various levels of social interaction).

6. The importance of the "absorbent mind," the limitless motivation of the young child to achieve competence over his or her environment and to perfect his or her skills and understandings as they occur within each sensitive period.

The phenomenon is characterized by the young child's capacity for repetition of activities within sensitive period categories (Example: exhaustive babbling as language practice leading to language competence). self-correcting "auto-didactic" materials (some based on the work of Jean Marc Gaspard Itard and Edouard Seguin)

4/4

Estée Lauder
Pioneered a whole new approach to producing and marketing cosmetics.

Pier Angeli
Paul McCartney
Idries Shah
Steffi Graf
George Bush
Doris Day
Diane Feinstein

6/9

Pablo Neruda
Ringo Starr
Freddie Laker
Kate Bush

Eva Braun
Vivaldi

Major General Orde Wingate, DSO and 2 bars

A British Army officer and creator of special military units in Palestine in the 1930s and in World War II. He is most famous for his creation of the Chindits, airborne deep penetration troops trained to work behind enemy lines in the Far East campaigns against the Japanese during World War II.

Wingate was flamboyant and outrageous in his personality, and was known for various eccentricities. For instance, he often wore an alarm clock around his wrist, which would go off at times, and a raw onion on a string around his neck, which he would occasionally bite into as a snack. He often went about without clothing.

In Palestine, recruits were used to having him come out of the shower to give them orders, wearing nothing but a shower cap, and continuing to scrub himself with a shower brush.

Sir John Templeton

The American-born British stock investor and philanthropist, had a deep interest in discovering more about life, especially the spiritual dimension, and founded the Templeton Foundation in 1987

Alexander Dubček

The Slovak politician, most famous for his attempt to reform the communist regime during the "Prague Spring" of 1968, was dedicated to the support of humanitarian causes.

Prince Charles
Betty Friedan
Janet Suzman
Tina Turner
Claude Monet
Rodin

8/7

Bjorn Borg

Edward Snowden
He made us all aware that there is no privacy on the internet and that governments and major institutions are collection data all the time when we use digital services.

Jerry Rawlings
The former military leader of Ghana known for his flamboyant leadership. On one occasion, Rawlings flew a MIG jet above Accra to indicate that he was still in charge.

Bill Withers
Jerry Hall

Juan Fangio
Great racing car driver, with a very flamboyant style.

Thomas Mann
Nietzsche's influence on Mann runs deep through his work, especially in Nietzsche's views on decay and the proposed fundamental connection between sickness and creativity. Mann held that disease is not to be regarded as wholly negative.

In his essay on Dostoyevsky we find: "but after all and above all it depends on who is diseased, who mad, who epileptic or paralytic: an average dull-witted man, in whose illness any intellectual or cultural aspect is nonexistent; or a Nietzsche or Dostoyevsky. In their case something comes out in illness that is more important

and conductive to life and growth than any medically guaranteed health or sanity…
in other words: certain conquests made by the soul and the mind are impossible
without disease, madness, crime of the spirit."

Salman Rushdie
John Constable

President Georges Pompidou
Georges Pompidou contributed to the modernization of Paris with the architectural
designs that originated under his Presidency

Marchais

Oriana Fallaci
Italian writer, journalist. Her interviews with national leaders were collected in
"Interviews with History" 1976.

Paul Gauguin

9/6

Pierre Trudeau
A traveler exploring other approaches and views about life. Flamboyant in style of
leadership.

Franz Liszt
Bill Gates
The Shah of Iran

Doris Lessing
English author, playwright. Her works concern people in social and political upheaval

3 WOOD CONTEXTUAL WINNING FIELD PERSONALITIES

ARE HIGH RISK TAKERS

Mahatma Gandhi
Salman Rushdie
Edward Snowden

Bill Gates dropped out of Harvard to pursue something that had no history and apparently no future

Jerry Rawlings lead a coup in Ghana

Tina Turner made an entire break from her marriage with nothing in place except the fact that it was time to leave

Janet Suzman standing against the Apartheid regime in South Africa

Alexander Dubcek leading the Spring uprising in Czechoslovakia against the Soviet regime.

Orde Wingate creating and leading the Chindits in Burma against the Japanese Army.

Freddie Laker starting the first discount airline where tickets were bought on the day of the flight.

T.E. Lawrence and his missions in the Middle East

George Jackson and his attempt to escape from a high security prison in America.

Juan Fangio and his style of motor car racing

SPURN RIGID FORMS OF EXPRESSION

Rabindragath Tagore's work introduced an entirely new way of writing in the Bengalese tradition. He brought a fresh lyricism and social content to his works.

The saxophone playing of John Coltrane and Wayne Shorter introduced entirely new ways of improvising on the instrument.

Bill Gates approaches to the computer made it available for personal use at home rather than an institutional device.

Prince Charles' outspoken comments about social issues, especially architecture, are outside of what is expected of him according to British Royal protocol.

Orde Wingate's Chindits unit created an entirely novel approach to military strategy.

Rodin's sculpture departed from the traditional themes of his time, moving in the direction of depicting the human body in a realistic manner.

Edward Snowden.

CHALLENGE ORTHODOXY

Tagore had been against the caste system in India and in favour of Indian self rule since the nineteenth century.

Pierre Trudeau introduced new constitutional legislation in Canada that went against the status quo.

Rodin initiated a change in the range of subject matter for sculptors

Edward Snowden viewed his role in his job to serve people and to be ethical in what he did.

TRAVEL BEYOND THEIR HORIZONS

Pablo Neruda became a diplomat in Burma and then in many South East Asian states, regions of the world that he had never heard about when growing up in Chile.

Orde Wingate journeyed into Sudan and lead the Ethiopian resistance against to the Italian invasion in World War II.

Gandhi's travels to South Africa, where he faced apartheid and organized forces against it.

Paul Gaugin settled in Polynesia where he embraced an entirely different lifestyle and adopted the eyes of the natives with his paintings and his social responses.

T.E. Lawrence travelled to the Middle East, and went down in history as "Lawrence of Arabia"

Edward Snowden became a global figure rather than an emploee of an American government agency living now in Russia.

HELP UNFOLD NEW SOCIAL AND POLITICAL RESPONSES

Pierre Trudeau and the intellectual journey he took with social, political and economic issues.

Alexander Dubcek and his flexibility in seeking to engage with the changing circumstances of his society.

Bill Gates moving from a tight-fisted hard-nosed business tycoon to creating the most generous charitable organization in the world.

Tagore with his strong opposition to the caste system and colonial rule, Tagore was his own ideologue about India's future direction and openly questioned Gandhi's views during India's colonial struggle, redefining his views as the situation changed.

Thomas Mann's changing political views from supporting

Kaiser Wilhelm conservatism against liberalism to democratic principles and the liberal left.

Doris Lessing moving from a Marxist position in her politics to a more humanistic spiritual view about social situations embracing Sufism over the last few years.

Edward Snowden opened up a whole new conversation about the internet and its issues and the transparency that can now serve society in a way that goes beyond commercialization and spying.

4 WOOD CONTEXTUAL WINNING FIELD APPROACHES

1/7
Tony Williams
Lord Atlee
Eric Clapton
Ursula Andress
Chris Evert
Hans Genscher
Shaquille O'Neal
Anwar Sadat
Helmut Schmidt
Henrik Ibsen
Kurt Waldheim
Ali Bhutto
Walter Mondale
Alexander Solzhenitsyn
Ben Webster

2/6
Geraldine Chaplin
Donald Sutherland
Patrick Ewing
Ernest Hemingway

Amy Vanderbilt

An American authority on etiquette. Published "Amy Vanderbilt's Complete Book of Etiquette" in 1952

Emily Bronte

English novelist. She is best known for her novel "Wuthering Heights" (1848) In childhood, after the death of their mother, the three sisters and their brother Patrick Branwell

Brontë created imaginary lands, which were featured in the stories they wrote.

6/2
Salvador Dali
Paul Gascoigne
Christopher Lee
Willie Mays
Rick Nelson

7/1

D.H.Lawrence

British novelist and poet. Published his poems about the natural world in "Birds, Beasts and Flowers". Lawrence is widely recognized as one of the finest travel writers in the English language. Wrote continuously on all ranges of interest. It is said he hand wrote 2,000 words daily.

Clive James
Margaret Trudeau

8/9

Kofi Annan
Jeremy Thorpe
Ravi Shankar
Audrey Hepburn
Glen Campbell
Karim Al Jabbar
Robert Burns

Derek Walcott

Nobel Prize for literature in 1992, his work dominates Caribbean literature.

Jerry Brown

Showed egalitarian responses to life, avoiding pomp and lavishness. Moved away from the palatial Governor's Residence when Governor of California.

Alan Bond

Jacques Brel

Multi-faceted expressions of life and its many aspects

Leonardo Da Vinci

9/8

Mother Teresa
Bill Clinton
Dustin Hoffman

Coco Chanel

French fashion designer. She revolutionized post-war women's fashions; subject of Broadway musical "Coco."

Beatrice Webb

Economist, sociologist, reformer. She articulated what co-operative societies were about, humanitarian concern for the less fortunate.

9/9

Bill Cosby
Stanley Kubrick
Linda Ronstadt
Emperor Haile Selassie of Ethiopia
Kenneth Starr
Benito Mussolini

Barbara Cartland

English novelist. "The Queen of Romance" was the world's top-selling romantic novelist; step-grandmother of Princess Diana.

4 WOOD CONTEXTUAL WINNING FIELD PERSONALITIES

ARE SKILLFUL AT CREATING NEW POSSIBILITIES

Anwar Sadat creating a Peace Treaty with Israel.

Jerry Brown's approach to politics is one of looking at other possibilities with energy, furthering scientific research to enhance the well-being of communities.

Hans Genscher's "Ostpolitik" rapprochement with the Soviet Union helped to ease the Cold War atmosphere in Europe.

Beatrice Webb's efforts in developing the co-operative banking and saving system in communities helped to empower those who were economically deprived to engage in meaningful financial transactions.

Mother Teresa's voluntary work helped alleviate a great deal of suffering in India and numerous Third World countries.

ARE COMMUNICATORS OF EPIC PROPORTIONS

Alexander Solzhenitsyn
Henrik Ibsen
Stanley Kubrick

Ernest Hemingway's work changed the structural approach of the 20th century novel.

Eric Clapton's song "Tears in Heaven" opened a way for himself and many others to come to terms with the tragic loss of a child.

EXPERIENCE LIFE CHANGING EXPERIENCES THROUGH TRAUMAS

Alexander Solzhenitsyn and his recovery from cancer triggered a call to Christianity and philosophical soul searching.

Eric Clapton's song "Tears in Heaven" was written following the death of his 4-year-old son Conor in 1991.

Emily Bronte's world changed after the death of her mother, and so began an imaginary construction with her sisters of lands and experiences in far away places.

D.H.Lawrence's persecution and censorship in England set him on his path of exploring other cultures and seeking other ways of living and writing about life.'

ARE IN PERSISTENT SEARCH FOR DEEP INNER MEANING

Ibsen's play "Peer Gynt" was consciously informed by the thinking of Kierkegaard.
Ibsen took challenging stances in much of his writing. In "An Enemy of the People", he chastised not only the right wing or 'Victorian' elements of society, but also the liberalism of the time. He illustrated how people on both sides of the social spectrum could be equally self-serving.
Alexander Solzhenitsyn's condemnation of Western materialism:
"...the human soul longs for things higher, warmer, and purer than those offered by today's mass living habits...by TV stupor and by intolerable music."

Stanley Kubrick's movies play upon the unconscious hinting at other ways and possibilities of looking at events.

Ernest Hemingway's on-going theme of having his characters show grow grace and ease whilst going through difficult experiences.

Anwar Sadat's search and pursuit of a Peace settlement with Israel.

DEEP RELATIONSHIP WITH TRADITIONAL VALUES

Ravi Shankar's music honours the musical traditions of Hindu India. He celebrates this joy with his audiences as he plays.

Henrik Ibsen was deeply inspired by the folk tales of Norway.

Alexander Solzhenitsyn admired and promoted the values of Monarchy and Church as being key to Russia's stability.
Dustin Hoffman embracing Judaism in later years as a source of inspiration.

PRACTICE IN DEPTH NOTE-TAKING IN GREAT DETAIL

Stanley Kubrick's control of his films, how they were released, alterations for different countries. The great detail he went into as regards how they were translated into other languages.

Da Vinci's numerous notebooks with endless sketches and drawings

Alexander Solzhenitsyn's large manuscripts with endless interviews and different angles on numerous topics.

5 EARTH CONTEXTUAL WINNING APPROACHES

1/9

Rita Hayworth
Eamon DeValera
Billy Graham
Cleo Laine
Roger Moore
George C. Scott

Joyce Brothers
US psychologist and author. She is a syndicated columnist, radio and TV show hostess. Brothers wrote "What Every Woman Ought to Know About Love and Marriage" (1984).

2/8

Fred Astaire
Tony Blair
Joe Cocker
Ho Chi Minh
Karl Marx

Marilyn Monroe
Michael Portillo

3/7
Brigitte Bardot
Peter Finch
Julio Iglesias
Kate Millet
Peter Sellers
Lech Walesa
George Gershwin
4/6

Samuel Beckett

Becket said: "I realized that my own way was in impoverishment, in lack of knowledge and in taking away, in subtracting rather than in adding."

James Knowlson, Emeritus Professor of French at the University of Reading and Beckett's authorised biographer, explains in "Damned to Fame: The Life of Samuel Beckett" (1996):

"Beckett was rejecting the Joycean principle that knowing more was a way of creatively understanding the world and controlling it...In future, his work would focus on poverty, failure, exile and loss -as he put it, on man as a "non-knower" and as a "non-carer"

Sandra Dee
John De Lorean
Janis Joplin
Hugh Gaitskill
Vladimir Ilyich Lenin
General Douglas MacArthur
Paul Newman
Jayne Mansfield
Barbara Streisand

Billie Holiday

On November 10, 1956, she performed two concerts before packed audiences at Carnegie Hall, a major accomplishment for any artist, especially a black artist of the segregated period of American history. Nat Hentoff of "Down Beat" magazine penned some of the liner notes for the 1961 album recorded during these two concerts.

He wrote of her performance: "Throughout the night, Billie was in superior form to what had sometimes been the case in the last years of her life. Not only was there assurance of phrasing and intonation: there was also an outgoing warmth, a palpable eagerness to reach and touch the audience. And there was mocking wit. A smile was often lightly evident on her lips and her eyes as if, for once, she could accept the fact that there were people who did dig her."

Hentoff continued "The beat flowed in her uniquely sinuous, supple way of moving the story along; the words became her own experiences, and coursing through it all was Lady's sound – a texture simultaneously steel-edged and yet soft inside: a voice that was almost unbearably wise in disillusion and yet still childlike, again at the centre.

The audience was hers from before she sang, greeting her and saying good-bye with heavy, loving applause. And at one time, the musicians too applauded. It was a night when Billie was on top, undeniably the best and most honest jazz singer alive."

6/4

Willy Brandt
Jennifer Capriati
Edgar Cayce
Doris Day
Dionne Warwick
Sharon Stone
Jack Kerouac
Al Jarreau
Ava Gardner
Alberta Hunter

7/3

Shirley Williams

Cat Stevens

Camilla Parker-Bowles

John Glenn

Sally Gunnell

Neil Armstrong

8/2

Jose Carreras

Lee Evans

King Farouk of Egypt

Charles Dickens

Vincent Price

John Steinbeck

George Washington

Andrés Segovia

9/1

Kusno Sosrodihardjo (Sukarno, first President of Indonesia)

Jack Le Pen

Sylvester Stallone

Jacques Cousteau

Che Guevara

Donald Trump

Harriet Beecher Stowe

Author of "Uncle Tom's Cabin" (1852). The novel depicted life for African-Americans under slavery. It reached millions as a novel and a play, becoming influential in both the US and Britain, and made the political issues of the 1850s regarding slavery tangible to millions.

The novel energized anti-slavery forces in the American North, while provoking widespread anger in the South. Upon meeting Stowe, Abraham Lincoln allegedly remarked "So you're the little lady who started this great war!"

Sun Yat-sen

Sun Yat-sen was a Chinese revolutionary and political leader. As the foremost pioneer of Republican China, he is ofter referred to as the Father of the Nation. His chief legacy resides in his developing a political philosophy known as the Three Principles of the People: nationalism, democracy, and people's livelihood. Sun was a uniting figure in post-Imperial China, and remains unique among 20th century Chinese politicians for being widely revered amongst the people from both sides of the Taiwan Strait.

5 EARTH CONTEXTUAL WINNING FIELD PERSONALITIES

BRING OUT THE BEST IN OTHERS

Billie Holiday: locate Billie singing "Fine and Mellow" in 1957 on YouTube. She's teamed with the best jazz musicians of the day and they are all eager to give of their best. This was consistently the case when musicians played with her.

Almost every musician who ever played with Miles Davis has acknowledged that he took their playing to another level and opened new possibilities for them.

Peter Sellers' presence on a movie set automatically lifted the theatrical presentations of the other actors and movie crew.

ARE SOCIAL REFORMERS

Charles Dickens' novels had an ongoing theme for social reform in England.

John Steinbeck persistently presented the injustices in American society in his work.

Harriet Beecher Stowe was told by Abraham Lincoln that her book "Uncle Tom's Cabin" had started the American Civil War.

Sun Yat Sen continually highlighted people's livelihoods as a key theme in his political policies.

HAVE A TIMELESS QUALITY OF EXPRESSION

Fred Astaire's dancing draws appreciation and interest even today .

On hearing Billie Holiday, you immediately realize that her songs are connected to human experiences and feelings in any period of time.

Miles Davis' trumpet playing, especially his "Concerto D'Aranguez" performance in Carnegie Hall, is simply beyond space and time.

The picture of Che Guevara in his beret speaks to all generations as an iconic image, regardless of political allegiances.

Sun Yat Sen's "Three Principles of the People" are accepted slogans on both sides of the Taiwan straits: both the government of the People's Republic of China and the Taiwanese government acknowledge these principles as part of their policies.

EXPRESS A NEW VISION, A NEW POSSIBILITY

Willy Brandt's seeking to break up the suspicion and Cold War politics between West Germany and Eastern Bloc countries when he was Chancellor.

Eamon De Valera brought a stability and focus to Irish politics out of a Civil War environment in Ireland at the time.

Jacques Cousteau brought the underwater world into people's lives, making them curious and engaged in this aspect of the planet.

Sun Yat Sen inspired many Chinese patriots and politicians to develop a stable China beyond the world of the feudal lords and barons.

Che Guevara sought to bring another possibility to Third World Countries through revolutionary activity.

ARE DILIGENT IN APPLICATION

Andrés Segovia's continuous development in his playing of the classical guitar.

Charles Dickens' continued focus on social issues with his writing.

Sun Yat Sen's political activities to unify China and create a stable life for its people.

Fred Astaire's constantly seeking ways to enhance his dancing ability.

Jacques Cousteau pursuing his interest in making the world under the sea more known by the general public. He created more than 100 underwater films.

6 METAL CONTEXTUAL WINNING FIELD APPROACHES

1/1

Jose Feliciano

Besides his musical skills and his Prolific output, Feliciano is known for his strong sense of humor. He constantly makes fun of people's reactions to his blindness, and has even played practical jokes on friends and family based on this. Once his then bass player, Ted Arnold, contrived to allow Feliciano to appear to be driving down a busy street, fooling the passing police.

On another occasion, during a show he said, "I was going to dedicate this song to Jackie Kennedy but I can't see her anywhere in the audience."

Kwame Nkrumah
Jessye Norman
Leo Tolstoy

Donny Hathaway
Moments of hesitancy and shyness

1/2

Van Morrison
Transcendental, prolific output, shyness

Whitney Houston
Paul Volcker
Wyomia Tyus
Althea Gibson
Wilt Chamberlain

2/1

Tracy Austin
Brian Clough
Dame Vera Lynn
Diana Ross
Gloria Swanson
Phil Donahue
Jimmy Swaggert

Lucretia Mott
Abolitionist, women's rights advocate First president of American Equal Rights Association

3/9

Mick Jagger
Barack Obama
Wole Soyinka
Jonas Savimbi

Frantz Fanon

Revolutionary: purification through violence. Freedom through violence creates a cathartic experience. Seizure of liberty by armed struggled. A new beginning would occur from this act. Individuals are trapped by society. A revolutionary ideology of the 60s and 70s. Free oneself by violence.

Giorgio Armani

Arthur Ashe

Standing for justice: being an activist against the South African apartheid regime

4/8

Galileo Galilei
Marian Anderson
Jimi Hendrix
Ludwig Erhard
Rudolf Steiner
Nina Simone
Jane Seymour
Otto Preminger
General Augustus Pinochet
Yoko Ono
Robert Mugabe
Larry King
Henry Longfellow

Lucky Luciano
Gloria Vanderbilt
Artist, painter, novelist

8/4

Betty Boothroyd
Scottie Pippen
Steve Kerr

Barbara Walters
TV Journalist

9/3

Albert Schweitzer
Jack Nicholson
David Bowie
Saddam Hussein
Colin Powell
Paul Cezanne
Farah Fawcett
Machiavelli

Freya Stark

Travel writer who explored areas of the Middle East that few Europeans at that time had ever visited, and most certainly no European woman.

6 METAL CONTEXTUAL WINNING FIELD PERSONALITIES

ARE SINGLE MINDED AND PERSISTENT

Kwame Nkrumah in his focus on Ghana's independence and African unity.

Van Morrison in his consistent and persistent efforts in exploring many dimensions of musical expression.

Albert Schweitzer and his missionary zeal in Africa.

Barack Obama's focus on becoming the first African-American President of The United States.

Ludwig Erhard's work on German economic policy which was already envisaged even when Hitler was in power. He was associated with resistance to Nazi rule and had economic plans in place for post-war Germany as early as 1942. He went on to become Economics Minister in Andenauer's cabinet and finally German Chancellor.

Brian Clough's management style with Nottingham Forest and Derby County whose fans, when he was manager, felt that the sky was the limit. He gave his players and fans the sense that any dream was possible.

HONOR ETHICAL PURSUITS

Leo Tolstoy and his religious fervor in living his life from Christian ethical values.

Albert Schweitzer honouring his ethical value system in going to Africa as a missionary.

Rudolf Steiner and his anthroposophical approach to life and its expressions.

Wole Soyinka in his plays, poems and novels articulating the need for a just and humanitarian approach for African governments to adopt in their governance.

Lucretia Mott was an advocate for the abolition of slavery in the 18th century. She was also a women's rights activist and the first president of American Equal Rights Association.

Tiziano Terzani and his travel journalism, always looking at it from a dimension of Hindu and Buddhist values. He embraced his terminal illness as a journey of becoming one with his mortality.

HAVE AN ALL-PERVASIVE INFLUENCE ON THEIR GENRE

Donny Hathaway's influence on R&B singers, composers and musicians has continued to grow over the years.

Leo Tolstoy's influence on Pacifism and nonviolence as a strategy for social change has see his work influence Mahatma Gandhi and Martin Luther King.

Van Morrison's impact on musicians, composers, song writers and singers of modern music.

Cezanne's influence on artistic expression, especially in the dimension of how "Space" is represented, continues to this day.

Whitney Houston's influence on R&B singers from Mariah Carey to Beyonce and many more, both male and female.

PRESENT A TRANSCENDENTAL QUALITY IN ARTISTIC PRESENTATION

Dame Vera Lynn's "We'll Meet Again" was the song of the British Armed Forces in World War II and triggers a nostalgia and spaciousness in the heart whenever it is heard and
sung.

Diana Ross' "Reach Out and Touch" brings this dimension to the fore in all of us.

Jose Feliciano's "Light My Fire"

Whitney Houston's "I Will Always Love You"

Jimi Hendrix's "Purple Haze" ("'scuse me while I kiss the sky")

Donny Hathaway "A Song for You" ("I love you in a place where there's no space or time")

Van Morrison's "Brown Eyed Girl"

Paul Cezanne's painting "Apples and Oranges" has that quality of stopping you wherever you are in your mind and fully connecting you with the apples and oranges on
that white table cloth.

Jessye Norman rendition of "Climb Every Mountain" in some way transfers you to that mountain that you wish to be climbing in your life.

Mick Jagger's "Sympathy For the Devil"

ARE ICONIC AND INIMITABLE PERFORMERS

Whitney Houston
Diana Ross
Van Morrison
Dame Vera Lynn
Jose Feliciano

Brian Clough as a soccer manager

Jack Nicholson
Jimi Hendrix
Mick Jagger

1/4
Michael Caine
Lord Louis Mountbatten
Kris Kristofferson

2/3
Dizzy Gillepsie
Oscar Wilde
Pablo Picasso
Michael Collins
Theolonius Monk
Luciano Pavarotti

3/2
Naomi Campbell
Laurence Olivier
Joe Namath
Jefferson Davis

Katharine Hepburn

US actress. Her films spanned 50 years including "The African Queen" (1951) and "On Golden Pond" (1982). In 1999, the American Film Institute ranked Hepburn as the greatest female star in the history of American cinema.
She won a record four "Best Actress" Oscars from eleven nominations.

4/1

Bob Geldof
Bud Powell
Sting
Marcello Mastroianni
T.S. Eliot
Jimmy Carter

6/6

Ella Wilcox
Poet, theosophist
John Lennon
Pele
Wayne Rooney
Dan Rather
Albert Camus
6/8

Babe Ruth
Yitshak Rabin
Christiaan Barnard
Boris Becker
Sri Chinmoy
James Dean
Richard Gere

Richard Pryor

Michael Jackson

Pierre-Auguste Renoir

Bruce Lee

Mikhail Gorbachev

Toni Morrison

Smokey Robinson

Rosa Parks

Adelle Davis

US nutritionist, author. She is best known for "Let's Cook It Right" (1947) and "Let's Eat Right to Keep Fit" (1954).

8/6

Natalie Wood

Carlos Santana

Jackie Onassis

Billy Eckstine

Jerry Rubin

Dag Hammarskjöld

Arnold Schwarzenegger

Richard Branson

Wallis Simpson

Mary Baker Eddy

US religious leader, writer. She founded the Christian Science Religious Movement and organized its first church in 1879.

Beatrix Potter

Author of children's books

7 METAL CONCEPTUAL WINNING FIELD PERSONALITIES

ARE SKILLFUL MARKETERS

Joe Namath New York Jets quarterbacks and his TV ads

Dr. Christiaan Barnard and his ways of promoting his work

Richard Branson

Arnold Schwarzenegger and his self promotion as a bodybuilder, movie star and politician

Bruce Lee's way of making martial art movies

Pablo Picasso's skill in hanging his paintings

Bob Geldof and his concerts for charity

ARE HUMAN RIGHTS ACTIVIST AND PROMOTERS

Bob Geldof
Jimmy Carter
Sting
Dag Hammarskjöld
Sri Chinmoy
Rosa Parks
Jerry Rubin

Pablo Picasso's painting "Guernica"

ARE EFFICIENT ORGANIZERS AND ADMINISTRATORS

Jefferson Davis

Dag Hammarskjöld

Hammarskjöld began his term as Secretary-General of The U.N. by establishing his own secretariat of 4,000 administrators. He set up regulations that defined their responsibilities. He was also actively engaged in smaller projects relating to the U.N. working environment: for example, he planned and supervised in every detail the creation of a "meditation room"

Arnold Schwarzenegger Governor of California

Richard Branson successful entrepreneur of the Virgin brand

Yitshak Rabin former Prime Minister of Israel

Lord Louis Mountbatten Admiral of the Fleet and Viceroy of India

Mary Baker Eddy and the creation of the Christian Science church

Bob Geldof's concert organizing skills

Michael Collins' organizing of the IRA cell system

ARE STRUCTURAL REFORMERS

Mikhail Gorbachev introduced the policies Perestroika and Glasnost to the Soviet Union which were the antithesis of what the Soviet Union was about.

Jimmy Carter

As president, Carter created two new cabinet-level departments: the Department of Energy and the Department of Education. He established a national energy policy that included conservation, price control, and new technology. In foreign affairs, Carter pursued the Camp David Accords, the Panama Canal Treaties and the second round of Strategic Arms Limitation Talks (SALT II).

Throughout his career, Carter strongly emphasised human rights.

Bruce Lee

The direction and tone of his films changed and influenced martial arts and martial arts films in Hong Kong and the rest of the world as well. Lee decided to develop a system with an emphasis on "practicality, flexibility, speed, and efficiency". He started to use different methods of training such as weight training for strength, running for endurance, stretching for flexibility, and many others which he constantly adapted. Lee emphasized what he called "the style of no style". This consisted of getting rid of the formalized approach which Lee claimed was indicative of traditional styles.

Rosa Parks' refusal to give up her seat to a white man because she was black on December 1 1955 sparked the Civil Rights Movement in America when the Montgomery bus boycott began.

Adelle Davis introduced a new way for Americans to look at their nutritional needs through her books.

Theolonious Monk and Bud Powell with the new innovations that they brought to the way that pianist played jazz. Some of these structural changes are still having their impact in jazz even today.

ARE EXPONENTS OF ENTERTAINMENT SKILLS

Michael Jackson

Carlos Santana

Richard Pryor

Sting

John Lennon

Luciano Pavarotti

Smokey Robinson

Bruce Lee

Beatrix Potter

Katharine Hepburn

Billy Eckstine

Babe Ruth

Dizzy Gillepsie

8 EARTH CONTEXTUAL WINNING FIELD APPROACHES

Jean-Baptiste Poquelin (Molière) is a 1/6, and his 8 CWF is very much present. As an 8 Earth CWF, Molière's antagonistic colours were green and purple. One of the most famous moments in Molière's life was his last, which became legendary: he collapsed on stage in a fit of coughing and hemorrhaging while performing in the last play he wrote, which had lavish ballets performed to the music of Marc-Antoine Charpentier and which was ironically entitled "Le Malade Imaginaire" (The Imaginary Invalid).

Molière insisted on completing his performance. Afterwards he collapsed again with another, larger hemorrhage before being taken home, where he died a few hours later, without receiving the last rites because two priests refused to visit him while a third arrived too late. The superstition that green brings bad luck to actors is said to originate from the colour of the clothing he was wearing at the time of his death.

8 EARTH CONCEPTUAL WINNING FIELD PERSONALITIES

TRANSFORM THEIR ESSENCE

Ted Roosevelt was born with health challenges yet took on the role of "Mr. Macho": boxing, safari hunting, soldiering, exploring.

Wilma Rudolph overcame asthma and polio as a child to win 3 Olympic Gold medals at the Rome Olympics.

Dame Tanni Grey-Thompson, The winner of 11 Paralympics gold medals

ARE AUTHENTIC SEEKERS

Aime Cesaire's writings, articulating the black man's experience in the Caribbean colonial setting. He totally challenged the status quo as to what was essentially important
in the existence of black people in the colonies.

Herman Hesse and his writings concerning the quest of connecting to one's authentic nature.

Vincent Van Gogh and the trials and tribulations he endured as he kept seeking and squeezing the essence of his creative juices in his paintings.

Boris Pasternak with his approach to poetry, revolutionizing the way that Russian poets wrote.

ARE TENACIOUS

John McEnroe and Pete Sampras' persistent efforts on the tennis courts.

Wilma Rudolph

Dame Tanni Grey-Thompson

Daley Thompson's athletic efforts

ARE READY TO TAKE A STAND

Vanessa Redgrave and her consistently outspoken political viewpoints.

Abraham Lincoln and his stand against slavery.

Aime Cesaire and his confrontations with colonial authorities about the dehumanizing conditions of the colonial experience for black people in The Caribbean.

Madame Roland during the French Revolution poignantly articulating her views and not compromising them even when facing the guillotine.

Sylvia Pankhurst and her uncompromising ideological positions reference Marxism, women's rights and Ethiopia.

Miriam Makeba and her uncompromising stand against the apartheid regime in South Africa.

ARE CREATORS OF MONUMENTAL ARTISTIC CREATIONS

Verdi for his operas

Alfred Hitchcock, Cecil B. De Mille and John Huston for their movies

Maria Callas for her operatic singing

Prince for his modern music performances and productions

Vincent Van Gogh for his paintings

Herman Hesse for his writing

Georgia O'Keeffe for her paintings

Boris Pasternak for his poetry and the novel "Dr. Zhivago"

Miriam Makeba

Judy Garland
Jeanne Moreau

Sylvia Pankhurst Women's rights, communist, "Ethiopian nationalist"

Marie-Jeanne Roland de la Platière (Madame Roland)
French revolutionary who was guillotined on trumped-up charges by other so-called revolutionaries

Dwight Stones
John McEnroe
Indira Gandhi
Pete Sampras
Abe Lincoln
Cecil B. De Mille
Werner Erhard
Alfred Hitchcock
Maria Callas
Charles De Gaulle
Eddie Murphy
Vincent Van Gogh
James Baldwin
John Houston
Daley Thompson

Aime Cesaire

Judy Garland

Herman Hesse

Wilma Rudolph

Meryl Streep

Prince

Evonne Cawley

Peter O'Toole

Boris Pasternak

Mark Spitz

Verdi

9 FIRE CONTEXTUAL WINNING FIELD APPROACHES

1/8

Leontyne Price, opera singer

Max Baer, boxer

Charles Barkley

Michael Jordan

Enrico Caruso

Jim Brown

Frédéric Chopin

Mia Farrow

Marvin Hagler

Glenda Jackson

Keith Jarrette

Bob Marley

Bette Midler

Sidney Poitier

Burt Reynolds

John Travolta

Jules Verne

Queen Victoria

2/7

Salvador Allende
Tom Cruise
Jean-Paul Sartre
Mario Cuomo
King Henry VIII
Lena Horne
The 14th Dalai Lama
Dean Martin
Robert Maxwell

3/6

Art Buchwald
Johnny Carson
Melina Mercouri
Margaret Thatcher
Joni Mitchell
François Mitterand
Janio Quadros

6/3

Joan Baez
Sir John Gieglud
Al Pacino
"Jersey Joe" Walcott
Placido Domingo
Norman Mailer
Franz Schubert
William Wordsworth
Yvette Mimieux
Ma Rainey, blues singer

7/2

Mark Zuckerberg
Brian Eno
Perry Como
Sean Connery
Sonny Rollins
Gary Snyder
Clint Eastwood
Martha Graham
Gil Evans
Jean-Michel Jarre
Davy Crockett

7/7

Le Bron James
Dirk Bogarde
Jean Claude Van Damme
Donna Summer
Stephen Sondheim
Steve McQueen
Spike Lee
Ali McGraw
Marvin Gaye
Helmut Kohl
Cesar Franck
Tiger Woods

8/1

Konrad Adenauer
Andrew Young
Joan Armatrading
Howard Cosell
Sir Alec Guiness
Ron L. Hubbard
Maynard Jackson
Elton John
Dorothy Lamar
Maurice Ravel
Michael Manley
Michael Schumacher
Tennesse Williams
Maurice White
Liv Ullmann
Wes Montgomery

Elizabeth Arden

Arden introduced modern eye makeup to North America. She also introduced the concept of the "makeover" in her salons. Arden collaborated with A. Fabian Swanson, a chemist, to create a "fluffy" face cream. The success of the cream, "Venetian Cream Amoretta", and the corresponding lotion, "Arden Skin Tonic", led to a long-lasting business relationship.

This revolutionized cosmetics, bringing a scientific approach to formulations. Some of her other innovations included creating foundations that matched a person's skin tone; creating the idea of the "Total Look" in which lip, cheek, and fingernail colours matched or coordinated.

Elizabeth Arden was also the first to make a cosmetics commercial shown in cinemas.

9 FIRE CONTEXTUAL WINNING FIELD PERSONALITIES

TRAILBLAZERS OF EPIC PROPORTION

Michael Jordan and his prowess on the basketball court: Jordan was given the nickname "Mr Air" because of his capacity to do things with the ball while in midair – almost as if he could fly.

Davy Crockett and his exploits since childhood that have now become an integral part of American legend.

Jim Brown still holds the record in American football for "rushing touchdowns", more than 44 years ago. He played by the philosophy 'Make sure when anyone tackles you he remembers how much it hurts" He was seldom pulled down when running with the ball, as he would carry the tackler with him as he ran.

Michael Schumacher holds the record of Formula 1 titles, with seven. No one has come close to equaling this record.

Elizabeth Arden's approach to marketing cosmetics in the early 20th century set the tone for how these products have been marketed since.

ARE DOMINANT LEADERS IN THEIR CHOSEN FIELD

Margaret Thatcher took on the Trade Unions and crushed them, and then when Argentina invaded the Falklands she declared war on Argentina without batting an eyelid.

Queen Victoria

Konrad Adenauer was the authority in German politics after World War II

Helmut Kohl was the longest-serving German Chancellor. He spent 17 years in the job.

Tiger Woods is without question the dominant force in golf today. In early 2009, USA Today reported on the dips in ratings for tournaments Tiger had won the previous season but missed because of a knee injury the next year. There was a 53 percent drop at the Buick Invitational, a 36 percent drop at the World Golf Championship-Bridgestone Invitational, a 55 percent drop at the PGA Championship, a 61 percent drop at the BMW Championship and a 47 percent drop at the Tour Championship. In a recent BusinessWeek story, Sam Sussman of Starcom Worldwide estimated that viewership for the last day of The Masters Tournament in April 2010 could rise more than 60 percent if Tiger makes it to the final round. There is little doubt that the business of golf improves exponentially when Tiger, the best player in the game, is active.

Francois Mitterand dominated the political landscape of France with his viewpoints and style during his presidency.

Davy Crockett is the most popular folk hero in American history.

Martha Graham is the mother of modern dance. All today's professional dancers acknowledge her influence on the art.

Le Bron James' appearance on the Basketball court, with his ritual of throwing chalk in the air, announces to the audience and players that he is on court and will dominate
the atmosphere of the game. This is exactly how it is when he comes on court.

Jim Brown remains a legend of the American Football field and it is a unanimous viewpoint that he is the greatest player ever.

Wes Montgomery has influenced every major jazz guitarist since he began playing, and has had an impact on many rock and blues guitarists.

LIKE WORKING UP A SWEAT

Michael Jordan and his exuberance on the basketball court.

Maurice White's performances with Earth, Wind and Fire are an ongoing dynamic presentation.

Donna Summer singing her songs, and people dancing to her disco music – sweating.

Le Bron James on the basketball court is all about going flat out and never stopping, driving himself continually to the basket.

ARE STRONGLY PASSIONATE ABOUT THEIR VIEWPOINTS AND EXPRESSIONS

Margaret Thatcher and her market economy views, and her whole approach to politics, was about passion.

Jean Paul Sartre's philosophical and political views was very direct, to the extent that he withdrew from many associates and organizations when they did not go along with his viewpoints. He refused a Nobel Prize for Literature.

Joan Baez's civil rights stance and songs for freedom and justice is all about her passion for these things.

Beethoven's "Ninth Symphony " is passion.

Ravel's "Bolero" is passion.

ARE CONSUMED BY WHAT THEY DO

Beethoven and his composing: even after he became deaf, he never gave up on composing and playing music.

For Keith Jarrett, playing the piano is an all-consuming experience, so that if someone in the audience sneezes he is thrown out from this "consumed" space.

Jules Verne was fully engaged with his need to discover and explore.

Bob Marley's continuous and consuming love affair with Reggae led to it becoming popular all over the world.

ARE PIONEERS

Bob Marley brought Reggae to the world.

Enrico Caruso the opera singer created the need to have a record player at home, as he was one of the first on the vinyl.

Jean-Michel Jarre created theatrical extravaganzas in the sky to go along with his music.

Joseph-Maurice Ravel wrote music for the one-handed pianist. He had a composition called "Concerto for the Left Hand".

Jules Verne pioneered science fiction writing. In 1863, Verne wrote "Paris in the 20th Century", a novel about a young man who lives in a world of glass skyscrapers, high-speed trains, gas-powered automobiles, calculators, and a worldwide communications network, yet cannot find happiness and comes to a tragic end. Verne's publisher, Pierre-Jules Hetzel, thought the novel's pessimism would damage Verne's burgeoning career, and suggested he wait twenty years to publish it.

Verne put the manuscript in a safe, where it was discovered by his great-grandson in 1989. It was published in 1993.

ENJOY MAKING THINGS VISUAL

Mark Zuckerberg's creation of Facebook, where images are the core aspect of this tool – the name says it all.

Jean-Michel Jarre's musical productions were all about adding a visual dimension to things.

Jules Verne's literary style was very much one of having you watch what he was describing. It is as though you are watching a movie when you read his books.

People who would never be interested in golf otherwise have tuned in to watch Tiger Woods. It is estimated that when he plays, TV ratings for the coverage are up an average of 40% globally.

The same thing was true of basketball when Michael Jordan was playing and also now, to a lesser degree, when Le Bron James is playing.

Breathe.

Let go.

And remind yourself

that this very moment

is the only one

you know you have

for sure.

Oprah Winfrey

CHAPTER 6

Global icons and how they manifest their contextual winning field

When we look at life, there seem to be some people who dominate their chosen field. If we think about this at all, we probably consider them to be lucky, impossibly talented, or born with a golden spoon in their mouths.

I have observed, however, that in the majority of cases there are patterns and personal habits of thought and action that these individuals have cultivated that have supported their success.

Let's take a look at some of these people now...

Here is something for you connect with regardless your status in life and also to move you out of the monster of just time management. Time Management is a monster when you do not have a connection with your Time DNA. Your Time DNA is your Contextual Winning Field. If you are dealing with Time without a connection to Your CWF, you are trying to get toothpaste back into the tube. It's messy.

Rex

CHAPTER 6

STEVE JOBS

A pioneer of the Global Computer Revolution, he created computer designs that connected directly with our sensory systems. The qualities of touch, sight and sound were inherently present in what he created. I have the feeling that Steve might have been working on some way to bring fragrance and taste into his devices. Maybe we will later discover that such ideas were part of his imaginative process of developing his cutting edge computer-based inventions.

He was the founder and CEO of Apple Inc., an interesting name for a computer company, inherently approaching computing if it were something that was biologically linked to our very existence. If we then reflect on the biblical story of the apple and Adam and Eve, he was working at subliminal levels of temptation, inviting us to come and partake of his products. Here was just one example of his gift as a skillful mass communicator.

In 1985, Jobs was fired by the Apple board by someone he had brought into the company: the board sided with his new appointee, and Jobs was gone.

He has often said that it was the biggest blessing in his life to be fired from a company that he had founded and which had a turnover of two billion dollars a year ten years later with four thousand employees.

For most people, such an experience would have crushed them, and had Steve Jobs simply given up and stopped trying, it would have been an understandable choice when we consider it from a rational viewpoint. Yet this was obviously not an option for him, as one of his core mantras was the line he got from Stewart Brand's last edition of the Whole Earth Catalog, "Stay Hungry and Stay Foolish". He often said that these were the guiding statements that he always wished for himself.

One can immediately understand that when operating with that mode, one is constantly searching for and looking to discover new possibilities.

So his next creation was NEXT, a computer platform development program company.

Interesting to look at the name of his next venture after being fired, "NEXT". As if his inherent trust and confidence was telling him: NEXT.

The lesson that one can learn from Jobs with this mantra is that it can function as the corner stone or motivation for a persevering visionary.

His exploration and study of calligraphy was something that Steve loved and he has acknowledge that doing this allowed him to create the subtle artistic typography of multiple type faces and proportionally spaced fonts that was the trademark of the Macintosh computer he was instrumental in developing. This seemingly effortless artistic expression has remained a signature feature of all Apple devices.

Obviously, Microsoft and others followed this with what they did...

This deep philosophical core in how Jobs looked at life was something that created a driven being. Steve Jobs constantly embraced his mortality.

Here are some quotes he made when addressing graduates from Stanford University in 2005.

"If today were the last day of my life, would I want to do what I am about to do today? When the answer is "NO" too many days in a row, I know I need to change something." "Remembering that you are going to die is the best way to avoid the trap of thinking you have something to lose. You are already naked. There is no reason not to follow your heart."

"Death is the destination that we all share: no one has escaped it."

"Death is most likely the single best invention of life. It's life-changing."

"If you live each day as if it is your last, someday certainly you will be right."

"If you have not found it yet, keep looking for what you love and don't settle. As with all matters of the heart, you will know when you find it."

Steve Jobs and how he lived has clearly shown us that he walked his talk.

We salute him for his Unconscious Mastery of his 1 Water Contextual Winning Field.

CORE CONTEXTUAL WINNING FIELD APPROACHES
1 WATER

1. OPERATING WITH CONFIDENCE IN THE INTANGIBLE DIMENSION OF LIFE
2. BEING AN IMAGINATIVE CREATOR
3. BEING A SKILLFUL MASS COMMUNICATOR
4. BEING A PERSEVERING VISIONARY
5. ENJOYING SEEMINGLY EFFORTLESS ARTISTIC EXPRESSION

OPRAH WINFREY

Oprah was born 29 January 1954 to an unmarried black teenage mother in one of the poorest areas in the state of Mississippi. This makes her 2 Earth as an Adult, and 9 FIre as a child, giving her the 1 Water CWF.

At the age of nine, several men (some of them relatives) raped her. At the age of fourteen, Oprah became pregnant: her son died in infancy.

Out of this extreme hardship and suffering, Oprah Winfrey rose to unimaginable heights. Sent to live with her father, a barber in Tennessee, she landed a job in radio while still in high school and began co-anchoring the local evening news at the age of nineteen.

At this early age, Oprah was expressing this persevering quality that her life could be better, in spite of her many trials and tribulations. Once she was so depressed that she wrote a suicide note to her good friend Gayle King, and yet she bounced out of that state of despair, trusting that the future (especially in the dimension of her career) was always going to be successful.

I have made this distinction about her career, which the whole world knows as an outstanding success. Speaking as someone who has worked as a body therapist for more than 40 years, I know that such traumas as she has been through and the imprints from her childhood and prenatal experiences are going to have a profound impact, and her earlier romantic hiccups and ongoing weight management issues arise from this. However, skillful mass communicator that she is, Oprah has taken the very compassionate approach of having her shows address lots of these life traumas she has experienced herself, and this truly seems to create a deep nourishment and healing for her and the millions who watch her shows globally.

This expresses her innate confidence that a better day is possible and achievable and that life has more to it than what is visible on the surface.

Her emotional ad-lib style eventually got her transferred to the daytime talk show arena, and after driving a third-rated local Chicago talk show to first place, she launched her own production company and became internationally syndicated.

Credited with introducing a more intimate confessional form of media communication, Oprah's eponymous, multi-award winning talk show became the highest-rated program of its kind in history and was nationally syndicated from 1986 to 2011. She has been ranked the richest African American of the 20th century, the greatest black philanthropist in American history, and was for a time the world's only black billionaire. She is also, according to some assessments, the most influential woman in the world.

Oprah's very spirit is an expression of the American Declaration of Independence: the inalienable right to life, liberty and the pursuit of happiness. Every breath that she takes is about manifesting that. Despite the shattering experiences of her childhood, Oprah's core belief in her rights as a free human being was never destroyed.

Her success is built on the philosophy that whatever challenges occur in life can be overcome. This is not packaging, spin or presentation: this is simply who she is. Plus, Oprah has a seemingly effortless style with her communication, it is in the same category as watching Picasso creating a painting or Miles Davis playing the trumpet. Oprah is elegant smooth art in action.

Oprah Winfrey has been called "The Voice of America", and she is an institution precisely because of the traumas and challenges she has overcome. In the late 20th and early 21st centuries, the expression "as American as apple pie" can easily be reworded to "as American as Oprah Winfrey".

Emotionally, Oprah has a very interesting Timeline when certain imprints ripen and manifest.

Take a look.

An Oprah Timeline

September 1981 Wrote a suicide note to her friend Gail King in a 1 Water Star month and year, although she did not attempt to take her own life.

March 1989 During a 1 Water Star month, Oprah faced the embarrassment of her half-brother's accusations of her abandoning him because he was gay and suffering from AIDS. She also had to deal with issues with her mother and half sister during this time.

1990 During this 1 Water Star year, Oprah endured a number of fresh challenges: She appeared on a list entitled "The Worst-Dressed Women on TV"

Her half sister sold the teenage pregnancy story to The National Enquirer

She hosted The Emmy awards for television shows, although she had no prize to receive herself.

Her boyfriend gave her an ultimatum to lose weight. Although the diet was an initial success, she eventually gained back most of the weight.

A TIP FOR OPRAH WINFREY

Anger is her Instinctive Emotional Response, and this can also manifest as intense impatience and frustration. When her heart is open and her disturbing emotions are out of the way, many of her audience and guests have commented on a healing energy they often feel from being in her presence. She is an alchemist, allowing unconditional love to flow to those around her.

On a transpersonal level, Oprah cannot control this. She can only let it flow. I suspect that she confuses the cellular system and emotions of her being when she attempts to then have this same energy as an emotional shield for self-protection.

This subtle dance with herself is one that can do wonders for her. Transition time is needed. Being receptive and aware of what arises for her in her dream state would be important, along with making sure that at these times, quality sleep becomes a major priority on her agenda. Obviously, preparing for sleep as if it is a very important journey she is about to take with her bedroom space being totally conducive for such a journey would further empower her as an alchemist.

The awareness of this poem may also facilitate opening more of these doorways to her.

> Smooth flowing waterfall ever present
> Yet never water to me.
> Deep blue waters pour into my present
> Embracing them clarity, conviction to be.
> Water touching whatever is present
> Endless Ganges persists blessing all to be.
> Effortless, elegant, persevering ever present.

Oprah Winfrey is a gift to the world and a woman who inspires all and sundry globally.

CORE CONTEXTUAL WINNING FIELD APPROACHES
1 WATER

1. OPERATING WITH CONFIDENCE IN THE INTANGIBLE DIMENSION OF LIFE

2. BEING AN IMAGINATIVE CREATOR

3. BEING A SKILLFUL MASS COMMUNICATOR

4. BEING A PERSEVERING VISIONARY

5. ENJOYING SEEMINGLY EFFORTLESS ARTISTIC EXPRESSION

PRINCESS DIANA

Princess Diana was born on 1 July 1961. This gives her 3 Wood as an adult, 1 Water as a child and the 2 Earth CWF.

She was born into an aristocratic family and arrived as a global personality when she became engaged to Charles, Prince of Wales, the heir apparent to Queen Elizabeth II, on 24 February 1981.

Diana carried an intense matriarchal energy, which was shown with the priority she gave to organising her life around her two sons rather than around what was expected of her as Prince Charles' wife. This core compassionate attitude extended to being passionately involved with charities that were catering for the dispossessed and alienated groups in society who were homeless or who suffered from debilitating sicknesses such as leprosy and AIDS.

She was very open about her personal life, and shared this revelation with the Premier of Newfoundland Brian Peckford in 1983: "I am finding it very difficult to cope with the pressures of being Princess of Wales, but I am learning to cope."

She was deeply committed to the banning of land mines, and her efforts in this area did create new legislation in Britain. She was a tireless supporter of The International Campaign to Ban Landmines (ICBL) with the organisation and its founder Jody Williams winning the Nobel Peace Prize in 1997 after Princess Di's death.

Her core desire was always to be "Queen Of People's Hearts," a desire she disclosed in a BBC interview in November 1995. Princess Di lived and embodied this in her life.

In so doing, she also became an iconic image creator that many women in public life seek to copy and emulate today. Yet, in the eye of the world there is only one Princess Di and oftentimes the media spots these emulation attempts and points it out.

Her divorce from Charles gave her the opportunity to live her life more freely on the world stage, and she commanded this presence like no actress or head of state had ever done. Interestingly, the only exception would be Nelson Mandela, who shares the same Contextual Winning Field pattern as Diana. What was truly inspiring about Diana's commitment to her work was that people and the media knew that this was not a marketing ploy on her part. This was a genuine heart space expression, and because of this she has become not just a cultural icon, but also a mythic one.

She engaged the collective unconscious of many people globally, thousands of whom went through a period of mental and emotional catharsis on her death. The tragedy of her death and how she died empowered this mythical dimension and one can say she has become a "phoenix arising from the ashes" as her image and memory on the world stage has grown exponentially since her death.

I suppose one could say that she surrendered her life to living from that compassionate desire of wanting to be "Queen of The People's Hearts", moving way beyond her own emotional pain and challenges and sincerely extended herself by service and example for the benefit of others. Princess Di has been dearly missed but vibrantly lives on in the hearts of people worldwide.

CORE CONTEXTUAL WINNING FIELD APPROACHES
2 EARTH

1.   HAVE THE CAPACITY TO BE INSPIRED FROM THE SPIRITUAL DIMENSION
2.   EXHIBIT A SINCERE CONCERN FOR HUMANITY
3.   BEING AN ICONIC IMAGE CREATOR
4.   ENJOYING THE CAPACITY TO OPENLY SHARE YOUR LIFE
5.   HAVING THE ABILITY TO RECREATE YOUR SELF

NELSON MANDELA

NELSON MANDELA was born 18 July 1918, which makes him a 1 Water as an Adult, a 3 Wood as a child and gives him the 2 Earth CWF.

He has become a global symbol for justice with an enduring resistance for human rights and personal dignity. His life has embodied this, and in dealing with his enemies and critics he maintains these same values to them. At times being criticized for his generosity of spirit by close friends and family, Mandela still maintains this attitude. The embracing of these values carries a very spiritual quality that often inspires the recipient of his generous compassionate nature. This is not to say that Mandela was a fool and would just give in when it came to principles of human dignity, nor to groups or nations that supported or went along with apartheid. He did keep his distance in such situations.

This ongoing concern for uplifting humanity has continued and his personal Foundation is a total dedication to this globally.

In his retirement from politics he has recreated himself as the global leader for the upliftment of all humanity. Anytime he appeared at events when he still travelled abroad, he was acknowledged, one can say, as the global monarch by all political, religious and social leaders. Plus, they all wanted him to attend their gatherings, as his presence would make it totally authentic and credible. In fact, not so long ago an international opinion poll found that if the world population had taken part in a presidential election, Mandela would have been the most popular choice.

Mandela has remained an icon for South African liberation and has now become a brand name for anything that is ethical in the world. He is also known for the fine quality clothes, which are individually tailored that bring a regal style with his presence. One has to remember that he came from a Royal family within the Xhosa tribe.

In interviews and in his biography Mandela has shared very intimate details about his life and his own personality shortcomings in a way that is very disarming and charming, in a way that you would wish to be in his company to experience these aspects of his personality.

The world has been inspired and left in awe by who he is and how he lives his life and we are blessed to be witnesses to who he is.

For moral courage and a mentor for character building he stands out in world history at the pinnacle of these attributes.

From a Contextual Winning Field viewpoint, it is very interesting to observe that on his official website he has chosen to use a yellow/orange type hue, which is the colour that supports his energy and creative expression.

CORE CONTEXTUAL WINNING FIELD APPROACHES
2 EARTH

1. HAVE THE CAPACITY TO BE INSPIRED FROM THE SPIRITUAL DIMENSION
2. EXHIBIT A SINCERE CONCERN FOR HUMANITY
3. BEING AN ICONIC IMAGE CREATOR
4. ENJOYING THE CAPACITY TO OPENLY SHARE YOUR LIFE
5. HAVING THE ABILITY TO RECREATE YOUR SELF

ICHIRO SUZUKI

Ichiro Suzuki was born October 22, 1973 and is a Japanese professional baseball player. He has the pattern of being a 9 Fire Adult and a 6 Metal Child. This gives him a 3 Wood Contextual Winning Field pattern.

Ichiro is a Japanese-born professional baseball outfielder. He currently plays for the New York Yankees, who he joined in 2012 having previously played for the Seattle Mariners. Originally, he was a player in Japan's Nippon Professional Baseball (NPB), where for nine years he played for the Orix Blue Wave in Japan's Pacific League. In 2001 he moved to the United States to play in Major League Baseball (MLB) for the Seattle team. He spent 11 seasons with the Seattle Mariners.

What is so special about Ichiro?

Well he has entered a sport where, had gone to a career guidance officer, they would have told him forget the idea. And most certainly do not even think about playing in America as you are much too small!

Well, Ichiro with the intense discipline learnt from his father, would have dismissed the idea "You can't" without pausing to even respond to such a limited view about what Ichiro can or can't do.

Ichiro stands 5 ft 9 1⁄2 (177 cm), and weighs 124 pounds (56 kg.) This height and weight indicates a small bone structure and even though he set many records during his school days playing baseball, still the Japanese professional baseball teams were reluctant to sign him due to his stature. Such orthodox projections about his capacity to dominate baseball were like water off a duck's back. What is truly beautiful and inspirational about his approach to baseball is that he wants to banish such views from people's minds, and he is deeply committed to the Ichiro Cup, a tournament that began in 1996. It is a 6-month long Boys' League tournament with over 200 teams, held in Toyoyama and surrounding cities and towns. Every year Ichiro attends the final game and the awards ceremony. This dedication to encouraging all young boys from this region of Japan to play basketball is a clear indication of his wanting to transform the restricted mindset about what can and can't be achieved because of height, weight and other considerations.

As he says, "I'm not a big guy and hopefully kids could look at me and see that I'm not muscular and not physically imposing, that I'm just a regular guy. So if somebody with a regular body can get into the record books, kids can look at that. That would make me happy."

When Ichiro was seven years old, he asked his father to teach him to be an excellent baseball player. Thus began a daily ritual with his father that consisted of throwing 50 pitches, fielding 50 infield balls and 50 outfield balls, and hitting 500 pitches, 250 from a pitching machine and 250 from his dad.

This intensity is still present with Ichiro's approach to his playing. He has a phenomenal work ethic of always arriving early to play for his team and for having a demanding warm-up routine along with his continual stretching exercises throughout the game. The bottom line with Ichiro is that he is focused on creating results for his team. He shies away from hype and marketing of what he hopes to achieve or how he would like the fans to respond or view his playing. He carries this budo spirit and dedication to his career and is not focused on how the fans will respond to his performance.

His whole approach to the game is unique: most coaches, when they first observe how he uses his body to do what he does are critical of it as it goes against the consensual view of how it should be done. He has created his own way of batting, pitching, catching. There is only one Ichiro.

The Japanese press has nicknamed him the "Hit-Making Machine" He has created such a core interest in Japan that over 150 Japanese photographers and journalists have been given media access to cover his career in America. His Japanese fans have been taking baseball tours, flying in and out of the US just to watch Ichiro's games. There is even a Sushi stand that sells an Ichiroll.

ICHIRO'S ACCOMPLISHMENTS

He is a ten-time Gold Glove winner. Ichiro is a ten-time All-Star selection from 2001 to 2010. His success has been credited with opening the door for other Japanese players to play in the US.

JAPANESE BASEBALL ACHIEVEMENTS

7 times NPB All-Star (1994–2000)
3 times Pacific League MVP 1994–1996)
7 times Golden Glove Award (1994–2000)
7 times Best Nine Award (1994–2000)
3 times Japan Professional Sports Grand Prize (1994–1995, 2001)
7 times PL Batting Champion (1994–2000)
5 times PL Safe Hit Champion (1994–1998)
5 times PL On-base Champion (1994–1996, 1999–2000)
Japan Series Champion (1996)
Major League Baseball in America
AL MVP (2001)

10 times MLB All-Star (2001, 2002, 2003, 2004, 2005, 2006, 2007, 2008, 2009, 2010)

MLB All-Star Game MVP (2007)

Twice AL Batting Champion (2001, 2004)

AL Stolen Base Champion (2001)

AL Rookie of the Year (2001)

3 times Silver Slugger Award (2001, 2007, 2009)

10 times Rawlings Gold Glove Award (2001–2010)

MLB Records:

262 hits in a single season

225 singles in a single season

Baseball Achievements:

4,000 hits combined in NPB and MLB

CORE CONTEXTUAL WINNING FIELD APPROACHES
3 WOOD

1. BEING A HIGH RISK TAKER
2. SPURN RIGID FORMS OF EXPRESSION
3. CHALLENGE ORTHODOXY
4. TRAVELLING BEYOND YOUR HORIZONS
5. HELP UNFOLD NEW SOCIAL AND POLITICAL RESPONSES

TINA TURNER

Tina Turner was born November 26, 1939, and is a singer, dancer, actress, and author.

She is a 7 Metal star as an adult and an 8 Earth star as a child. This gives her the 3 Wood Contextual Winning Field pattern.

Tina was the wife of Ike Turner, and they were a very popular duet back in the sixties and early seventies. She left Ike Turner in 1976, escaping a very abusive relationship, and divorced him.

As she shared in her biography, this was a big risk for her to take as she was not moving to a new circumstance, she was escaping from something she knew that she had to leave, and this was the only impulse: nothing else mattered.

She left with 36 cents in her pocket and a gas station credit card. She has stated that her practice of the Buddhist mantra Nam Myo Ho Ren Ge Kyo is what kept her going in these challenging times: TIna is a practitioner of the Soka Gakkai Buddhist lineage.

This was totally outside of her upbringing, as she grew up a Baptist: her parents and relatives belonged to the Baptist denomination. Tina was travelling far beyond her horizons with her choice of religious practice.

Tina went from being a black R&B singer to being an actress when she played the role of The Acid Queen in the movie "Tommy" to great success. In 1985, she played Auntie Entity in the movie "Mad Max: Beyond Thunderdome". She eventually moved away from R&B altogether, and became known as the Queen of Rock: she has sold more tickets than any other solo performer in the world. She has won 8 Grammys and her performances on stage are the most dynamic of any entertainer. The only one who carried this same level of dynamism on stage was the late James Brown.

Tina has, by her style of singing, what she sings, and how she sings it become an inspiration for women everywhere as an assertive, independent woman who still carries a feminine charm. On stage, she is her own person and delivers as only she can: her performances are unique and authentically who she is and what she is about. She has relinquished her American citizenship and become a Swiss citizen.

Her top 3 songs are: "Proud Mary", "River Deep, Mountain High" and What's Love Got To Do With It?"

Tina Turner is in a class of her own, and unconsciously manifests the 3 Wood Contextual Winning Field pattern. She expresses all these aspects in living her life and are in fact at the core of her being who she is.

CORE CONTEXTUAL WINNING FIELD APPROACHES
3 WOOD

1. HIGH RISK TAKERS
2. SPURN RIGID FORMS OF EXPRESSION
3. CHALLENGE ORTHODOXY
4. TRAVEL BEYOND THEIR HORIZONS
5. HELP UNFOLD NEW SOCIAL AND POLITICAL RESPONSES

ALEKSANDR ISAYEVICH SOLZHENITSYN

Aleksandr Isayevich Solzhenitsyn (11 December 1918 – 3 August 2008) was an eminent Russian novelist and historian.

He was 1 Water as an adult and 7 Metal as a child, giving him the 4 Wood CWF.

"For the ethical force with which he has pursued the indispensable traditions of Russian literature" Solzhenitsyn was awarded the Nobel Prize in Literature for 1970.

Solzhenitsyn was a Titan. After going through his challenges and traumas, he remained committed to Russian nationalism and its Christian Orthodox value system. He held that the pursuit of these ideals were in the best interest for Russia. He harked back to the rule of the Tsars, and said it was much better for Russia in comparison to the communist state of the Soviet Union.

In looking at Solzhenitsyn's worldview, he had a predilection for glorifying Russia's past and its Tsarist and Orthodox Christian position of life. He then embodied these views and wrote from this philosophical and historical perspective. He became totally disillusioned with the Soviet Union while fighting in the Second World War, so much so he wrote to a friend about it. The letter was intercepted and under Stalin's rule this was an offence that led to incarceration. His time in prison deepened his contempt for the Soviet system of government and fostered his nationalistic sentiments about Russia and the greatness of its culture and values. His definitive statement about the failure of the Russian revolution and its traumas for the people and the society is that "Men have forgotten God: that's why all this has happened. "

He was very thorough with his research, and collected enormous amounts of data to make his point, and what made his statements credible was that he suffered many years imprisonment, going through major illnesses during these times behind bars.

This episode of his life was the basis of his novel "Cancer Ward", as he suffered from cancer whilst incarcerated.

This deep strength of character and moral fibre that are constant themes in his writings and views of life seems to be at the core of his recovery: the determination not to give in, of not surrendering his spirit which was something he never gave up. There was a tenacious quality of pursuing other approaches to life other than what surrounded him, especially when it did not match up to his view of things. This characteristic was fiercely expressed even when Solzhenitsyn was living in the West. He was critical of the egocentric attitude that was prevalent in America, and the lack of moral fibre in facing challenges.

His early years were traumatic, as his father was killed in a hunting accident when his mother was pregnant with him. She never remarried. She was an educated woman and encouraged her son's academic interests. In his childhood they had to keep secret the fact that his father had been an Army Officer in the Tsar's army, as this would create a major displacement for them where they lived.

Solzhenitsyn's writings about life in the Soviet Union were a major factor in the lack of trust that wide cross-sections of western society had about the Soviet Union and its policies. Most certainly, he did get the ear of many Western leaders with his pronouncements, and this contributed to certain policy changes in British, American and German political attitudes to the Soviets. In my view, one has to look beyond his political positions and connect with his relentless seeking for authenticity about what he wrote, and it came from what he had experienced with all the difficulties and life-threatening situations he encountered as he lived his life.

The long, bitter-cold winters, the hardships of the Gulags, and yet through it all his diligence of creating, taking notes, looking at it all through his own values. Then, to stand as a Colossus in the world with an uncompromising attitude that was a continuous longing for a past that he cherished, although he somehow never found a way to come to terms with how the world had changed. Though seemingly anachronistic, he nevertheless had a deep concern about life and the honouring of certain values that he constantly upheld in his life and writings.

His was an extremely rare presence in modern life, one who dedicated himself to his writings with no shortcuts or marketing ploys about it. He constantly delivered with clear statements about his values. He was an Unconscious Master of the 4 Wood Contextual Winning Field pattern.

Solzhenitsyn's most notable works are:

* One Day in the Life of Ivan Denisovich
* The First Circle
* Cancer Ward
* The Gulag Archipelago (3 volumes)
* The Red Wheel

Solzhenitsyn also wrote poetry ("Prussian Nights" was such a volume) as well as many political pamphlets.

CORE CONTEXTUAL WINNING FIELD APPROACHES
4 WOOD

1. BE SKILLFUL AT CREATING NEW POSSIBILITIES
2. BE A COMMUNICATOR OF EPIC PROPORTIONS
3. EXPERIENCE TRANSFORMING YOUR LIFE
4. BE IN PERSISTENT SEARCH FOR DEEP INNER MEANING
5. DEEP RELATIONSHIP WITH TRADITIONAL VALUES
6. PRACTICE IN DEPTH NOTE-TAKING IN GREAT DETAIL

MERCEDES SOSA

Mercedes was born July 9th 1935. This makes her a 2 Earth Star as an adult and 6 Metal Star as a child, giving her the 4 Wood Contextual Winning Field pattern.

Sosa was born in San Miguel de Tucumán, in the north western Argentine province of Tucumán, of Mestizo, French, and Amerindian ancestry.

She brought these indigenous qualities to her singing, and one hears it especially with her rendition of "Duerme Negrito", and also with "Todo Cambia" where she would often accompany herself with a traditional drum of the First Nation People of the Americas. As one listens to her rendition of this song, it has the capacity of melting you into a trance state. This arises from her voice and her way of surrendering herself to the lyrics and at the same time allowing her spirit to bend it into other dimensions in this yielding. This deep relationship to honouring traditional music from the Americas was something that Mercedes embraced. She was a key player in what was known as the "Nueva Cancion" ("New Songs") movement . This movement spread throughout Latin America and had a folkloric orientation along with left-wing politics.

The period 1976 to 1979 was a very traumatic one for Mercedes. The military junta of Jorge Videla came to power in 1976 and this created a very oppressive atmosphere in Argentina, especially for someone like her with her political leanings. Her second husband died in 1978. At a concert in La Plata in 1979, Sosa was searched and arrested on stage, along with all those attending the concert. She was only released because of international pressure on the Argentine junta. She was then banned from Argentina and moved to Europe, initially to Paris before settling in Madrid. She was widely known as "La Negra", "The Black One". She was also known as "The Voice Of The Voiceless Ones".

These trials and tribulations did not dent her spirit, as she continued to be popular in Argentina and returned in 1982, holding a massive concert some months before the collapse of the junta. She dug deeper into her left-leaning political orientations and pursued this with a relentless enthusiasm. Her voice is consistently calling out for another way, arising from a fervent heart for a more caring world. The deep inner meaning that Mercedes keeps searching for in her songs and how they are rendered is for everyone to have the opportunity to celebrate life.

Mercedes had sold out concerts at Carnegie Hall and the Coliseum in Rome. As one can see on YouTube, she has a global following with some of her songs having over 9 million hits as of December 2013. Reuters reported her death by saying she "fought South America's dictators with her voice and became a giant of contemporary Latin American music".

She was a UNESCO Goodwill Ambassador for Latin America and the Caribbean. She recorded 40 albums, and her signature song was "Gracias a La Vida".

After her death on October 4th 2009, three days of official mourning was declared by the Argentine government.

Mercedes won the Latin Grammy Award for Best Folk Album in 2000 for "Misa Criolla", in 2003 for "Acústico" and in 2006 for "Corazón Libre", as well as many international awards.

CORE CONTEXTUAL WINNING FIELD APPROACHES
4 WOOD

1. BE SKILLFUL AT CREATING NEW POSSIBILITIES
2. BE A COMMUNICATOR OF EPIC PROPORTIONS
3. EXPERIENCE TRANSFORMING YOUR LIFE
4. BE IN PERSISTENT SEARCH FOR DEEP INNER MEANING
5. DEEP RELATIONSHIP WITH TRADITIONAL VALUES
6. PRACTICE IN DEPTH NOTE-TAKING IN GREAT DETAIL

BILLIE HOLIDAY

Billie Holiday was born April 7, 1915 giving her the pattern 4/6   5 Earth CWF.

In 1937 she had her sole number one hit "Carelessly".

However, her signature song was "Strange Fruit", a protest song about the horrors of the lynching of black people in the segregated southern American states. In her first performance with Artie Shaw at the Waldorf Astoria Hotel ballroom, she demanded that she had to open the show with "Strange Fruit". This was the first time that a black female singer had appeared with a white band in America. Billie Holiday stood for change and was expressing a new vision, a new possibility and did this continuously in her artistic career.

One needs to know that Billie Holiday's beginnings were horrifically traumatic: her mother was a teenage single mother who was rejected by her parents and who had to leave home and live by herself because she was pregnant. Billie's mother was seldom around as she had to find jobs and Billie was left with her mother's half-sister. She often did not go to school as a young girl and before she was 10 years was arrested for playing truant and sent to a Catholic Reform school. She was released after 9 months, into her mother care. She then worked long hours at her mother's restaurant. At the age of 11, she was raped. She dropped out of school and worked in a brothel running errands when she was 12. When she was 14 her mother moved to Harlem in New York and Billie joined her and she and her mother worked as prostitutes in a brothel. She was arrested a few months later and she and her mother went to prison. This is the pain that is at the core of Billie's life and heart space.

Yet in spite of it and her self-destructive drug habit, Billie Holiday was an inspiration to singers world wide and remains an epic entertainer whose phrasing and style have been copied or more accurately they've TRIED to copy her, but you know, there's always something missing. We all know that, because once you've heard Billie Holliday sing, you remember it forever. This is the timeless quality that is a trademark of her singing.

Frank Sinatra had this to say about her in 1958:

"With few exceptions, every major pop singer in the US during her generation has been touched in some way by her genius. It is Billie Holiday, who was, and still remains, the greatest single musical influence on me. Lady Day is unquestionably the most important influence on American popular singing in the last twenty years."

Her genius, especially as a jazz singer, can be heard in the piece "A Sailboat In The Moonlight". In this piece, it's almost impossible to separate her voice from the sound of the saxophone. It is not one of her favourites, but I have not heard any singer who has kept that pitch and phrasing throughout a song, keeping it the same as that of the wind instrument musicians. Keep in mind that Billie was never trained or instructed by anyone as to how she should sing, neither did she go to any school to learn musical arranging.

Many musicians and singers have claimed that she shaped the expression of jazz and modern music. The way she manipulated her innovations as she sang was a masterpiece of artistry.

Though her voice faded from the drug abuse it suffered, I think everyone is enthralled and astounded by the diligence she brought to her singing right to the end of her life. She held that control of phrasing and pitch as she languidly sang a little bit behind the beat and invoked in what she sang emotions no one else has brought to a song.

All musicians when they played with her have acknowledged that they wanted to play their best when they were accompanying her. One can clearly see that this is present on the YouTube video clip "Fine and Mellow". She is accompanied in this song by Jazz Royalty. Illustrious names like Ben Webster, Lester Young, Gerry Mulligan, Coleman Hawkins, Roy Eldridge. When you watch this, you can feel this competition with each other and themselves to squeeze the best out for her. This was always there when she sang. Lady Day's legacy lives on, and each year it seems to get stronger the more we hear her.

CORE CONTEXTUAL WINNING FIELD APPROACHES
5 EARTH

1. BRING OUT THE BEST IN OTHERS
2. BE SOCIAL REFORMERS
3. HAVE A TIMELESS QUALITY OF EXPRESSION
4. EXPRESS A NEW VISION, A NEW POSSIBILITY
5. ARE DILIGENT IN APPLICATION

MILES DAVIS

THE CREATIVE GENIUS OF "KIND OF BLUE"

Miles Davis was born May 26, 1926. He was a 2 Earth personality as an adult and an 8 Earth personality as a child. His Contextual Winning Field was the 5 Earth Field.

I have approached Miles' Contextual Winning Field impact from a different perspective than the other personalities. His creation of the album "Kind of Blue" has had such an impact on the world (and on musicians in particular) that I am sharing it here as a case study of the deeper dimensions of what the Contextual Winning Field paradigm is about. With this album, Miles manifested his genius: it ripened into this spontaneous action called "Kind of Blue". Of course, there was a lot of other work that Miles and his sextet had done before. But as his pianist Bill Evans said, this album happened with the first take.

Miles was known for bringing out the best in his musicians. All of the musicians became famous from certain pieces that they played on this album. Paul Chambers opening with his bass lines on "So What" had never been done before. No piece ever opened with a bass! It expressed a new vision, a new possibility for musicians. Miles pioneered this. Miles changed the way that people looked at music and experienced it. The very name of some of the musical scores enrolled people in hearing it that way – independent of what was played and how it was played. The name "Kind of Blue" speaks volumes about the everyday lives of people in the modern world. "So What" has its own voice, along with the term "All Blues", and even "Blue in Green" said something to people and their lives.

Miles brought a diligence and focus of application to the task, and to nail each track consistently in first takes was totally awesome. Plus the crowning glory of this album is that it has continued to sell an average of 5,000 albums globally each week. In October 2008, it was certified to have sold a total of more than 4 million copies. The sound of Miles' trumpet has a timeless quality, and the "Kind of Blue" album confirms this nicely with its continuing sales.

Of course, one can wax lyrical about other wonderful albums and concerts that Miles Davies created. However,, in my humble view his collaboration with Gil Evans and their Carnegie Hall concert in May 1961 where he played Concerto de Aranguez stands out as a true masterpiece. So far, to my ears the first eight minutes of this performance is the best piece of live 20th century music I have ever heard.

MODAL MUSIC AND MILES

Modal music, which is what "Kind of Blue" is about, came about from a question that George Russell asked Miles years before the album was made. Russell asked Miles what his musical aim was, to which Miles replied, "I want to learn all the changes." This set Russell on the course that became his life work, and he created The Lydian Chromatic Concept.

Since Miles obviously knew all the changes, Russell surmised that what he meant was he wanted to learn a new way to relate to chords. Hence Miles was instrumental in triggering the creative process in George Russell, enabling him to become the creator and founder of modal music.

KIND OF BLUE

In 1959, Miles spearheaded a way of approaching music that was completely different, and in many ways shifted how people listened to music. He did this by moving outside of the regular scale structures and patterns, and engaging something called modal expression.

Davis was primarily a jazz musician. In the album "Kind of Blue", he transcended all these boundaries.

We can see the result of this transcendence in the fact that music lovers of all persuasions around the world still listen to this album. It is THE definitive Jazz album. We have already mentioned that Miles' Contextual Winning Field is the 5 Earth Star. The expressive aspects of the 5 Earth Star in its Contextual Winning Field expression are timelessness, inimitability, a quality of balance and stabilization and a provocative tone that creates a sense of curiosity.

"Kind of Blue" was recorded in 1959 in two sessions. The first session was on March 2nd 1959, a 2 Earth month in a 5 Earth year. Two Earth is his adult Star, and a 2 Earth month would have his adult 2 Earth Star in the central 5 House, supporting him in stabilizing and integrating the whole modal approach to Jazz music, which in some ways defines the album. Davis ran the final session on April 22nd. April was a 9 Fire month, placing his adult 2 Earth Star in the 7 Metal House, the House of The Harvest. "Kind Of Blue" has remained in a state of harvest ever since.

Here is what Bill Evans, Miles' pianist in these recordings, had to say about what occurred during the recording:

"There is a Japanese visual art in which the artist is forced to be spontaneous. He must paint on a thinly stretched parchment with a special brush and black water paint in such a way that an unnatural or interrupted stroke will destroy the line or break through the parchment. Erasures or changes are impossible. These artists must practice a particular discipline, that of allowing the idea to express itself in communication with their hands in such a direct way that deliberation cannot interfere.

The resulting pictures lack the complex composition and textures of ordinary painting, but it is said that those who see well find something captured that escapes explanation. This conviction that the direct deed is the most meaningful reflection has, I believe, prompted the evolution of the extremely severe and unique disciplines of the jazz musician. Group improvisation is a further challenge. Aside from the weighty technical problem of collective coherent thinking, there is the very human, social need for sympathy from all members to bend for the common result. This most difficult problem, I think, is beautifully met and solved on this recording.

As the painter needs his framework of parchment, the improvising musical group needs its framework in time. Miles Davis presents here frameworks, which are exquisite in their simplicity and yet contain all that is necessary to stimulate performance with sure reference to the primary conception.

Miles conceived these settings only hours before the recording dates and arrived with sketches, which indicated to the group what they should play. Therefore, you will hear something close to pure spontaneity in these performances. The group had never played these pieces before, and without exception the first complete performance of each was a take." Bill Evans.

"Kind Of Blue" always seems to have more to give. If we keep listening to it, again and again, throughout a lifetime, well maybe that's because we sense there's still something more, something not yet heard. Or maybe we just like paying periodic visits to heaven.
-Robert Palmer Music critic

As Herbie Hancock said: "Name me some music where you don't hear echoes of it!" Suffice it to say that to this day, it would not be uncommon to overhear a bandleader say; "now on this ballad, I want a "Kind of Blue" feel". It remains a standard by which other jazz recordings are measured.

CORE CONTEXTUAL WINNING FIELD APPROACHES
5 EARTH

1. BRING OUT THE BEST IN OTHERS
2. BE SOCIAL REFORMERS
3. HAVE A TIMELESS QUALITY OF EXPRESSION
4. EXPRESS A NEW VISION, A NEW POSSIBILITY
5. ARE DILIGENT IN APPLICATION

DAME VERA LYNN

Dame Vera Lynn, DBE born 20 March 1917, is widely known as "The Forces' Sweetheart".

She is a 2 Earth star as an adult and a 1 Water star as a child. This gives her the 6 Metal Contextual Winning Field pattern.

She was the voice of Britain during the Second World War. Yes, there was Churchill, but musically and uniting families it was the sincere words and songs from Dame Vera on Radio that kept spirits up.

What is interesting about her life is that she never wanted to sing. It was her mother who encouraged her, and as a child Vera embarked on her singing career to boost the family income.

Vera Lynn left school at 14, and made a name for herself as a young teenager singing in the working men's clubs in London.

When Vera was 15, she answered a BBC advertisement for a singer for their dance band. She applied, had an audition but the letter she received a few days later told her that her voice was not suitable for broadcasting.

It's very interesting that despite her young age, such comments did nothing to deter her. A persistent single-minded tenacity was already present. She had an interesting motto, which was: "I like it when things go wrong, because then it's then a challenge."

Another core aspect of her personality is that she chose her own songs, as the lyrics had to feel comfortable for her.

She persisted with this throughout her career. When the War began in 1939, things initially closed down in the entertainment industry in Britain. In 1940, there was a poll among the British Armed Forces as to who was their favourite singer and Vera Lynn came out on top. In 1940 the desire for entertainment was very great as people needed some escape from the misery they were facing, big bands were back in business and Dame Vera was a popular feature. In 1941 she suggested to the BBC that she do a radio program for the Armed Forces personnel, and so began her "Sincerely Yours, Vera Lynn" radio show in November 1941. This was totally new, as nothing like this had been done before, where a public medium, the radio, was used for personal messages. The show was very popular and she received more than 2,000 letters a week from listeners at home and abroad. This is when "We'll Meet Again" became her signature song.

It was not plain sailing for her with this show, as the Director General and some of the conservative elements in the BBC were very critical of it, claiming that it would weaken the men on the front with all these sentimental songs and messages. Vera Lynn dismissed this as rubbish, as the messages from her listeners indicated otherwise and the majority of the general public and the Armed Forces loved the show, including the top brass of the military. Their view was that it was good for troop morale.

Vera Lynn toured operational areas and sang for the troops in many locations, including Egypt, Burma and India.

She brought another quality to her singing and entertainment, especially with the troops. She was caring, sincere and compassionate. She was not a sex symbol, tantalising the troops. She was the transcendent link with her feminine quality which united the boys with their families, wives and sweethearts back home. The lyrics of "We'll Meet Again" do carry that transcendental quality:

We'll meet again don't know where don't know when
But I know we'll meet again some sunny day
Keep smiling through, just like you always do
Till the blue skies drive the dark clouds far away
So will you please say hello to the folks that I know
Tell them I won't be long
They will be happy to know that as you saw me go
I was singing this song
We'll meet again don't know where don't know when
But I know we'll meet again some sunny day

Obviously thousands of soldiers, sailors and airmen lost their lives in the war yet as you hear her singing, she is implicitly suggesting that even if they die in battle, they will be linked again with their loved ones on the other side. This continuity was there, and her voice brought power to it. Interestingly enough, after the war she was the first British singer to have a No 1 hit in America with "Auf Wiedersehen, Sweetheart" 1952.

Auf Wiedersehen is a German expression for goodbye. In the early 1950's the memories of the war and the Germans bombing of England were still vivid for the British public, yet she used German words to create a popular song, indicating that Vera Lynne was not about bitterness, but about compassion and bringing love and care for loved ones wherever and whoever they are, again illustrating her transcendental quality in whatever she did.

Her popularity still remains intact, as at the age of 92 in September 2009, Lynn became the oldest living artist to make it into No. 1 in the British album chart with "We'll Meet Again: The Very Best of Vera Lynn".

Dame Vera Lynn and the honouring of ethical standards go hand in hand. She is a true doyenne in manifesting unconsciously the qualities of the 6 Metal Contextual Winning Field.

The songs most associated with her are "We'll Meet Again", "The White Cliffs of Dover", "A Nightingale Sang in Berkeley Square" and "There'll Always Be an England".

The music and lyrics of "We'll Meet Again" were written by Ross Parker and Hughie Charles.

CORE CONTEXTUAL WINNING FIELD APPROACHES
6 METAL

1. BEING SINGLE MINDED AND PERSISTENT
2. HONORING ETHICAL PURSUITS
3. HAVING AN ALL-PERVASIVE INFLUENCE ON YOUR GENRE
4. PRESENTING A TRANSCENDENTAL QUALITY IN ARTISTIC PRESENTATION
5. BE AN ICONIC AND INIMITABLE PERFORMER

KENICHI HORIE

Kenichi Horie was born September 8, 1938 in Osaka. This gives him a pattern of an 8 Earth star as an adult and a 4 Wood star as a child. His Contextual Winning Field pattern is 6 Metal.

Kenichi is a Japanese solo yachtsman. He rose to prominence when he became the first person to sail solo across the Pacific Ocean in 1962. He made this 5,300 mile journey from Osaka, Japan to San Francisco in a 19 foot (5.8 metre) plywood sail boat, "The Mermaid". He knew no one, had no connections in America and had no plan of how to get back home, not to mention that he could barely speak English.

He left Osaka on May 12, 1962 and arrived in San Francisco on Sunday, August 12, 1962.

How did such a journey come about? Kenichi says:

"A burning passion for the sea gripped me. Maybe it was then that the Pacific began to beckon to me, inviting me to dream of a boundless open sea to sail" (This quote comes from his book "Kudoku".)

This passion took him beyond the everyday limits that most of us experience. However, in his own inimitable way Kenichi embrace dsuch a challenge because he wanted to do it. It was as simple as that.

We get a glimpse of his persistent single-minded attitude to life with this statement of his: "If you make up your mind to do something -if you are determined to do it- there is only one way to go about it. Work out your own ideas on the general course you are going to follow and stick to them: stand on those basic ideas and assume responsibility for your actions. You yourself have to work out what you think is the best plan, and carry it out to the end. You may make mistakes, there may be details in your plan that could have been improved upon by relying on someone else's advice, but basically it has to be your personal responsibility to conceive and carry out the project."

This attitude of honouring the mind and adopting the goals that have been triggered within the heart is very much how Kenichi approaches life. It therefore comes as no surprise to learn that he espouses environmental concerns with his solo sailing journeys. This has become a dominant theme with his sailing. In 1985 he sailed from Hawaii to Chichijima off the coast of Japan in a solar- powered boat.

Then in 1992, to 1993 he sailed from Hawaii to Okinawa in a pedal -powered boat.

In 1996 Kenichi took his environment-friendly commitment to another level when he created a solar powered boat made from recycled aluminium. He sailed this boat from Salinas, Ecuador to Tokyo. This distance of 10,000 miles (16,000 km) took him 148 days. The journey earned him a place in The Guinness Book of World Records for the fastest-ever crossing of the Pacific in a solar powered boat.

He took his recycling efforts into new creations with his Malt Mermaid II catamaran that was made from 528 beer kegs welded in 5 rows end-to-end. The rigging was made from recycled plastic bottles. He sailed in this boat in 1999 from San Francisco to Japan.

In 2008 he became the first person to sail in a vessel that was only propelled with ocean wave power.

Wave power took him on this 7,000 kilometres (3780 nautical mile) journey from Hawaii to Wakayama port in 110 days all alone. He averaged a speed of 1.5 knots per hour (1.7 mph, 2.735 kph.)

Just in case you get the impression that he is caught in some functional warp of only creating recycled sailboats that are nature powered, you will have a big surprise when you read the poetic and romantic requests he made when he donated his first sailboat, "Mermaid", to the San Francisco Maritime Museum.

He presented a commemorative tray on which the following is inscribed:

"I would like for you - the people of this beautiful City of San Francisco, the City that I shall remember as the one that made my youth such a colorful event - to accept my most loved one, "The Mermaid." My entire youth was spent in carrying on a conversation with her. She was the one who gave me courage when I was lonely and weak. She is a lonely heart, too. I tried to encourage her when she was depressed by talking to her about the Golden Gate Bridge that she had longed to see. Both of us were tied together strongly by trusting each other with the impatience of young lovers. The two of us left Nishinomiya Port on the night of May 12, 1962. Putting entire confidence in the strength of this little lover of mine, we set sail into the vast ocean ahead of us...It is unbearable for me, now, to leave her behind in a foreign country. It pains my heart terribly to think that she is left behind alone. You will please be kind to her. Please be kind to my tired lover: please be good to her. Although she may look a bit unpainted and pale, I don't doubt that she is most serenely contented inside. She is injured all over, but she is immersed in the memories of her 94 days on the high seas. Will you please speak to her, this lonely heart, when you are moved to do so. And will you please listen to her talk about the stars, the waves and the skies over the Pacific Ocean. And recall for a short moment, if you will, the deed of a young Japanese, who loved the yacht and the United States of America."

Kenichi Horrie is an unconscious master of the 6 Metal Contextual Winning Field, he encompasses all the attributes that symbolize this pattern.

CORE CONTEXTUAL WINNING FIELD APPROACHES
6 METAL

1. BEING SINGLE MINDED AND PERSISTENT
2. HONORING ETHICAL PURSUITS
3. HAVING AN ALL-PERVASIVE INFLUENCE ON YOUR GENRE
4. PRESENTING A TRANSCENDENTAL QUALITY IN ARTISTIC PRESENTATION
5. BE AN ICONIC AND INIMITABLE PERFORMER

AUNG SAN SUU KYI

Born 19.6.1945, She is a 1 Water personality as an adult and a 4 Wood personality as a child. Her Contextual Winning Field is the 7 Metal Field.

She came from a powerful Burmese family: her father had formed the modern Burmese army and led the country to independence from The British, but he was assassinated before Burma's independence was finalized.

Tragedy has been the backdrop of her life since childhood. Her father was assassinated when she was two, one of her brothers drowned when she was about 5 years old and prior to this her sister had died when she was just a year old. As if that were not enough, her US-based, American citizenship holding elder brother, Aung San Oo, is a major critic of his sister, and brought a lawsuit against her when she was under house arrest in 2000. He claimed half a share in the family home where she was housed during this detention period. After the death of her mother in December 1988, Aung San Suu Kyi was placed under house arrest, with odd variations on the same theme, until 2010. Her husband Dr Michael Aris died in March 1999. When he was diagnosed with cancer in 1997 and wanted to return to Burma, the junta refused him entry. The last time she saw her husband was Christmas 1995. I highlight these traumas that surround her because despite all that on her shoulders she carried the political torch of human rights and democracy for Burma, a country that has been rife with political and social turmoil over the last century, creating phenomenal suffering and tension among different social and ethnic groups during this time. In 1990, her NLD political party won the elections and would have claimed some 80 per cent of the parliamentary seats but the political junta nullified the election.

Within this sea of turmoil and tragedy Aung San Suu Kyi kept and maintained the following approaches to living her life:

SKILLFUL MARKETER

By simply being who she is, she is packaging and marketing the brand "Aung San Suu Kyi". This is not a spin-doctored scheme to grasp your attention: this is simply the authentic expression of the truth of who she is.

HUMAN RIGHTS ADVOCATE

"It is not power that corrupts but fear: fear of losing power corrupts those who wield it, and fear of the scourge of power corrupts those who are subjected to it."

Her definitive political statement.

EFFICIENT ORGANIZER AND ADMINISTRATOR

Aung has been the General Secretary of The National League For Democracy since 1988 and since then has held that mantle and inspired the masses of Burmese people to follow her path.

STRUCTURAL REFORMER

"Government leaders are amazing: they're the last ones to know what the people want."

She is known to operate from an inclusive approach in dealing with the political and social challenges facing Burma, especially in dealing with the power of the military, and seems receptive to approaching the challenges that face her country with a willingness to learn from other countries. It needs to be pointed out that some of this gloss and shine she had with her views has been dimmed by the recent religious violence that has arisen between Buddhists and Muslims, although she has not gone so far as condemning their actions outright.

EXTENSIVE ENTERTAINMENT SKILLS

Aung is an accomplished pianist and is known to have the capacity to move people with her music.

She won the Nobel Peace Prize in 1991, the award being accepted by her two sons.

CORE CONTEXTUAL WINNING FIELD APPROACHES
7 METAL

1. BE SKILLFUL MARKETER
2. BE HUMAN RIGHTS ACTIVIST AND PROMOTER
3. BE A STRUCTURAL REFORMER
4. BEING AN EXPONENT OF ENTERTAINMENT SKILLS
5. BE AN EFFICIENT ORGANIZER AND ADMINISTRATOR

PETER MINSHALL

Minshall was born 16 July 1941, making him an 8 Earth adult personality and a 6 Child personality combination. This gives him the 7 Metal Contextual Winning Field profile.

Peter Minshall has dominated the Trinidad and Tobago Carnival celebrations with his epic designs and creations over the last three decades. He has done this in such a way that he has transformed how Mas is played in Trinidad. He pioneered the use of movement and dance with his portrayals of the King and Queen of his band where these very intricate and sometimes massive creations move and tell a story by their actions that leaves you with no doubt about the authenticity of what the king or queen is portraying at the Dimanche Gras show in Port of Spain on the Carnival weekend.

He has shifted what the mindset of Carnival is about, or can be about. Of course, most bands don't engage with such deep and riveting issues in their Carnival portrayals, yet that door to engage with profound aspects of the cultural psyche of people living in Trinidad and Tobago is so startlingly provocative that Minshall brings you right to the threshold, showing you where we currently are and what we are facing: plus, he has this ability to weave these core issues and play it out in front of your very eyes on stage, on the street, in a theatre performance or stadium where you see a master entertainer weave his magic around you. This weaving keeps you on the edge with what is coming next, what is going to happen,, and most times something does happen. The times when nothing happens, he has still magnetized you and some impression is then etched on your mind

Minshall's depictions have a way of enrolling and mesmerizing the mind space of human beings. When you look at how his Carnival portrayals move, or the colours (or lack of colour) of Mas players, it takes you somewhere else in your imagination. A new journey of the mind begins. As the Trinidadian photographer Roy Boyke has said, "It is doubtful if the work of any single individual has had so searing an impact on the consciousness of an entire country."

His mastery has caught the attention of the global market to such an extent that he has been invited to create the opening ceremonies for 2 Summer Olympics: Barcelona in 1992 and Atlanta in 1996. He also created the opening ceremony for the Pan American Games in 1987 in Indianapolis and the 1994 Football World Cup in Chicago. This interest in his creativity has also extended to the opening ceremonies of the 2002 Winter Olympics in Salt Lake City and the 2007 Cricket World Cup in Jamaica.

His authenticity arises from that core need to reform the human psyche so that it engages with life from compassion. Yet, Minshall is never naive in his approaches of representing the human condition and its limitations, as he has this unnerving way of presenting his work so that it often feels like a bayonet in the nostrils with no apologies being made as to how you experience it.

Then there are the portrayals of how human beings, from time immemorial, have wrestled with the challenges of good and bad and ways of overcoming life's many obstacles, and these sometimes happen in triplicate.

Minshall rivets people's imaginations when he starts a presentation... where is this going? What's next? How will this develop? These epics are diligently organized and administered, and when the moment comes with all the suspense that surrounds it he delivers his masterstroke.

Of course within his many creations he does show a lightness and joyousness that clearly indicates his capacity to celebrate life, as exuberant laughter, movement and having fun is also present.

Minshall is The Master Marketer of his creations. The kaleidoscope of his creations, once seen, remain etched in your mind like the tablets of Moses.

His heart space and concern for the human condition sees him engaging in creations that clearly show that he is a human rights activist and promoter. His "Adoration of Hiroshima" in Washington D.C. in 1985 is just one example. This again shows his aptitude of never missing an opportunity to get to the core of the matter: in this case, bringing it home in all its tragic horror with not much said, just mesmerizing sounds and macabre death images moving in the streets to a drone sound.

This was another one of his "bayonet up the nostrils" moments with no sign of Peter Minshall on the streets of Washington but everyone from Trinbago would know: the only person in the world who could have created this, without a shadow of doubt, was Peter Minshall. And he delivered this in Washington DC, the place where the decision to bomb Hiroshima had been made.

Minshall is consistently, in all his works, howling for the rights of human beings to be honored and cherished with every part of his expression, movement and posture. The weaving of this thread is always present.

He has the beat of the global DNA of all human beings as he breathes life into his new creation.

I say this based on the immediate connection that people from other cultures have, the second they see his representations. This has occurred many times when I share a YouTube clip of his work with friends from Central Europe, Asia, Africa- people who have never seen Trinidad Carnival yet within a second of seeing Minshall's mastery are enrolled and engaged in what he is presenting. The pulse of their DNA resonates with his artistic designs.

It goes without saying that any year when Minshall brings out a band for Carnival, that band is full, and many Trinidadians, wherever they are in the world, return to Trinidad to play Mas with his creation that year. Plus, there are people from all over the world who, on discovering that Minshall will have a band at Carnival, also come to play Mas with him. It is a total understatement to call Peter Minshall a Skilful Marketer. He has taken that definition to a whole new level: he is a global magnetic marketer. No one is ever bored with seeing his creations: some are TOTALLY shocked, some feel disgust towards it and express certain defensive responses. There are also many who are transformed, and with their eyes, ears and skin are going through a whole new experience of living, just from watching and being present with what is before them as his Mas band streams across their senses.

Readers, this is Peter Minshall, a truly Universal Icon of the 7 Metal Contextual Winning Field Attributes.

CORE CONTEXTUAL WINNING FIELD APPROACHES
7 METAL

1. BEING SINGLE MINDED AND PERSISTENT
2. HONORING ETHICAL PURSUITS
3. HAVING AN ALL-PERVASIVE INFLUENCE ON YOUR GENRE
4. PRESENT A TRANSCENDENTAL QUALITY IN ARTISTIC PRESENTATION
5. BE AN ICONIC AND INIMITABLE PERFORMER

VINCENT VAN GOGH

Vincent Van Gogh was born on the 30th March 1853. 3 Wood as an adult, 4 Wood as a child. 8 Earth was his CWF.

In February 1888, van Gogh settled at Arles, where he painted more than 200 canvases in a fifteen month period. During this time he sold no pictures, was living in poverty, and suffered recurrent nervous crises, with hallucinations and depression. He became enthusiastic at the idea of founding an artists' co-operative in Arles, and towards the end of the year Gaugin joined him.

However, as a result of a quarrel between them, van Gogh suffered the crisis during which he cut off his left ear (or part of it), an event commemorated in his "Self-Portrait with Bandaged Ear".

In May 1889, he went at his own request into an asylum at St Rémy, near Arles, but continued during the year he spent there with a frenzied production of tumultuous pictures such as "Starry Night". He executed 150 paintings besides drawings in the course of this year. In 1889, his brother Theo married and in May 1890 van Gogh moved to Auvers-sur-Oise to be near him, lodging with the patron and connoisseur Dr. Paul Gachet.

There followed another tremendous burst of strenuous activity and during the last 70 days of his life he painted 70 canvases. However, his spiritual anguish and depression became more acute and on 29 July 1890 he died from the results of a self-inflicted bullet wound.

His period of confinement in the asylum was one of the most prolific of his life. He seemed to gain strength and stability from the secure and structured routines of daily life there. "Starry Night" and "Cypresses" are two very well-known masterpieces that date from this period.

Vincent Van Gogh was born on the 30th March1853, a 4 Wood star month in a 3 Wood Star year. His disturbing emotion was Grief, and Van Gogh embraced that experience fully as he struggled throughout his life with poverty, horror at the suffering he saw around him and deep bouts of depression.

Yet in spite of it all, Van Gogh was a prodigious painter in one period towards the end of his life, painting 70 paintings in 70 days. Like Picasso, Van Gogh was driven by the grief he felt, and what he brought to his paintings was the eye of the observer, with no judgments implied by his art, except for his use of colour.

He used colour to express himself more forcibly. This comes from expressing his 8 Earth Wisdom Star. The core essence of the 8 Earth Contextual Winning Field is the Observer who connects with deep feelings of Loving Kindness in its most generous expression. He represented this eloquently with his "Potato Eaters" painting.

Even with his frightening mental anguish, Van Gogh held on to a structure and a capacity to observe the world and keep producing timeless art with a warm, heartfelt compassion. He kept doing whatever it took to keep drawing on those resilient reserves of the 8 Earth Contextual Winning Field. He was engaging the core essence of his being to create the alchemy of Transformation of himself through what he had put on the canvas. He was uncompromising with himself, and regardless of his depression he was committed to creating his paintings. He pursued this vision continuously as he kept seeking the ultimate in his artistic expression. One has to remember that Vincent never sold a single one of his paintings, yet this did not inhibit his drive to create and manifest his destiny. The 8 Earth Contextual Winning Field is the most resilient and tenacious of all the Contextual Winning Fields.

CORE CONTEXTUAL WINNING FIELD APPROACHES
8 EARTH

1. TRANSFORMING YOUR ESSENCE
2. BE AN AUTHENTIC SEEKER
3. BE TENACIOUS
4. BEING READY TO TAKE A STAND
5. BE A CREATOR OF MONUMENTAL ARTISTIC CREATIONS

WILMA RUDOLPH

"Wilma Rudolph's courage and her triumph over her physical handicaps are among the most inspiring jewels in the crown of Olympic sports...She was speed and motion incarnate, the most beautiful image ever seen on the track."

Jesse Owens

Wilma Glodean Rudolph (June 23, 1940 – November 12, 1994) was an American athlete and an Olympic champion. Rudolph was considered the fastest woman in the world in the 1960s.

She was born prematurely on June 23, 1940 in St. Bethlehem, Tennessee, weighing 2.04 kg (4.5 lbs.). Most of her childhood was spent in bed: she suffered from double pneumonia, scarlet fever and later contracted polio. After losing the use of her left leg, she was fitted with metal leg braces when she was 6 years old.

"I spent most of my time trying to figure out how to get them off," she said. "But when you come from a large, wonderful family, there's always a way to achieve your goals."

Rudolph grew up in a poor family, the 20th of her father Ed's 22 children (from two marriages). Although she never shared a home with all her siblings and half-siblings at once, there were still plenty of brothers and sisters to serve as "lookouts" if she mischievously removed her braces. Rudolph was out of her leg braces by age 9.

Growing up in the South before the end of segregation, Rudolph attended an all-black school, Burt High School, where she played on the basketball team. A naturally gifted runner, she was soon recruited to train with Tennessee State University track coach Ed Temple.

Rudolph became an all-state player, setting a state record of 49 points in one game.

Temple made the girls run an extra lap for every minute they were late to practice. Rudolph once overslept practice by 30 minutes and was made to run 30 extra laps. The next day she was sitting on the track 30 minutes early.

Although Rudolph had never even heard of the Olympics until high school, she attended the Olympic trials in Seattle and qualified for the 1956 Olympics in Melbourne, Australia at the age of sixteen, as a high school junior. The youngest member of the American team, she was excited to go on her first airplane flight. At Melbourne, she was eliminated from the 200-metre event and did not make the final, but she ran the third leg of the 4×100 metre relay and won a bronze medal.

The Olympic Games, Rome, 1960

During her senior year of high school, Rudolph underwent a routine physical and found out that she was pregnant. Her parents and coach supported her, and she finished high school and kept up with her training as much as she could. A month after graduating, she gave birth to a daughter, Yolanda. Her parents, who wanted her to attend college, took care of the baby until she was able to do so.

Rudolph's Olympic victories were even more amazing, because on the day before the 100 metre semifinal, she stepped in a hole and twisted her ankle. It swelled and became painful, but Rudolph ran anyway, and won her semi-final.

At the 1960 Rome Olympics, Rudolph became "the fastest woman in the world" and the first American woman to win three gold medals in one Olympic Games. She won the 100 and 200 metre races and anchored the U.S. team to victory in the 4 x 100 metre relay, equalling and breaking records along the way.

When she returned from Rome, Tennessee Gov. Buford Ellington, who was elected as "an old-fashioned segregationist," planned to take charge of her welcome home celebration. Rudolph said she would not attend a segregated event.

Her homecoming parade in Clarksville was attended by over 40,000 people, and was the first racially integrated event in the history of the town—at her insistence, since she refused to participate in the segregated event that the white town officials originally proposed.

Rudolph's parade and banquet were the first integrated events in her hometown of Clarksville.

A track and field champion, she elevated women's track to a major presence in the United States. As a member of the black community, she is also regarded as a civil rights and women's rights pioneer.

Rudolph especially inspired young African-American female athletes. Most notable was Florence Griffith-Joyner, the next woman to win three gold medals in one Olympics (1988).

"It was a great thrill for me to see," Rudolph said. "I thought I'd never get to see that. Florence Griffith-Joyner: every time she ran, I ran."

Bob Kersee, husband and coach of Jackie Joyner-Kersee, said Rudolph was the greatest influence for African-American women athletes that he knows. His wife went further: "She was always in my corner," said Joyner-Kersee, winner of six Olympic medals. "If I had a problem, I could call her at home. It was like talking to someone you had known for a lifetime."

CORE CONTEXTUAL WINNING FIELD APPROACHES
8 EARTH

1. TRANSFORMING YOUR ESSENCE
2. BEING AN AUTHENTIC SEEKER
3. BEING TENACIOUS
4. BEING READY TO TAKE A STAND
5. BEING A CREATOR OF MONUMENTAL ARTISTIC CREATIONS

JONI MITCHELL

Joni Mitchell was born in Canada November 7, 1943. This gives her the pattern of a 3 Wood Star as an adult and a 6 Metal star as a child which then creates the 9 Fire Contextual Winning Field pattern.

She is a Colossus on the world stage as a creative personality who transcends all musical genres in such a way that she fits no boxes.

However, she has this capacity of opening an emotional door through which you can see yourself, to come home to yourself, in a very surprising way: it is a direct honesty of vulnerability. This is the cornerstone of what she does: she has pioneered that approach, created the opportunity for others to move from one style of singing into a whole new area without any need for justification or explanation. In a way you can say it is an organic unfolding of her creative process: she is really inviting her listeners to see themselves in the lyrics she is singing. Joni has pursued this process relentlessly with her songs: she truly is a trailblazer of monumental proportions.

When you think about Joni Mitchell, you will discover no one who follows in her footsteps and is doing or attempting to do what she does. Obviously she is viewed in total awe in the world of music and singing. The names of singers and musicians who are inspired by her work and who have performed her songs and played her music is the A-list of today's performers and artistes. Prince, James Taylor, Kanye West, Annie Lennox, Caetano Veloso, Elvis Costello, Wayne Shorter, Charles Mingus, Herbie Hancock and Jaco Pastorius to name only a few.

Joni has won 8 Grammys. Her most popular song, "Both Sides, Now", has almost 600 different recorded versions as of 2013.

What is the difference that Joni brings to her songs and singing?

She makes things visual for the listener. As she openly says "I apply painting principles to music." Painting is what she is about; this is how she approaches her song writing and music: she even paints most of her own album covers. Her album "Turbulent Indigo" is dedicated to the memory of the artist Vincent Van Gogh, again indicating her link with visual imprints in her song writing and singing. She won a Grammy Award for this album in 1994, and it was Pop Album of the year.

She is totally passionate about her life, and does not mince words in articulating her viewpoints. She is totally critical about the delusional celebrity obsession that has taken over the music industry and modern life. She has no computer or answer-machines at her home, as she believes that electronic pollution corrupts biological systems and is a further extension of our insanity as a species, and that we will pay a terrible price for it.

Joni's creative process consumes her. We get a sense of this and how open and vulnerable she leaves herself from her song "Chinese Café" from the 1982 album "Wild Things Run Fast". The song contains the lyrics: "Your kids are coming up straight / My child's a stranger / I bore her / But I could not raise her." She was singing about her daughter, who she had to put up for adoption as she was unable to look after the child, and the social stigma that went with having a child out of wedlock in 1965 was very much that of a terrible criminal. As she often says, "I had no ambition or drive to be a singer. I sang in the clubs to get money to survive and when my daughter was born she went into an adoption home."

When she reconnected with her daughter in 1997, she lost all interest in song writing: as she was finally able to communicate with the person who she wanted to talk to, the need to communicate with the world dropped away.

She has been viewed as the most important and influential female recording artist of the late 20th century. The magazine Rolling Stone has named her as one of the greatest songwriters ever.

What is not so widely known is that Joni has struggled with health challenges throughout her life but says very little about it, as the creative process is what she loves. Her bottom line mantra is "You are on your own. Let's face it."

CORE CONTEXTUAL WINNING FIELD APPROACHES
9 FIRE

1. BE DOMINANT LEADER IN YOUR CHOSEN FIELD
2. ENJOY WORKING UP A SWEAT
3. BE STRONGLY PASSIONATE ABOUT YOUR VIEWPOINTS AND EXPRESSIONS
4. BE CONSUMED BY WHAT YOU DO
5. BE A PIONEER
6. ENJOY MAKING THINGS VISUAL

MICHAEL JORDAN

Michael Jordan was born 17th February 1963 in Brooklyn New York. Jordan is a 1 Water star personality as an adult and an 8 Earth as a child, giving him the 9 Fire Contextual Winning Field.

Jordan dominated American basketball in the 1990s and became a global icon, with people all over the world switching on their TVs, just because of him, to watch the Chicago Bulls play. People who never had an interest in basketball were fascinated by what he did and how he did it. Oftentimes, people from as far away as Japan would make a trip to Chicago just to watch him play. His popularity was that vast. Jordan's style of play was inspired by another famous basketball player, Julius Irving, better known as Dr J who emphasised leaping movements above the rim of the basketball net.

Jordan's emulation of these moves and his seemingly long time in the air led him to be named Air Jordan and also "His Airness".

Once, when asked about the secret of his success, Jordan replied "Sweat". When he was playing for the Chicago Bulls, he trained every morning on his own basketball court for an hour to build up a sweat.

On the basketball court, Jordan expressed himself with phenomenal passion and energy. His dominance of the court was so potent that in the closing seconds of a game where the Chicago Bulls needed 2 or 3 points to win, Jordan would be handed the ball and given free rein. His success rate at these times was close to 100 per cent.

He was consumed by everything he did, and pioneered a level of marketing Jordan as a brand that had not been seen before. It is claimed that the Jordan Brand accounted for one billion dollars of Nike revenue in 2009. The Air Jordan trainers were a shoe that had a slick marketing strategy, especially the humorous ad with Spike Lee as Mars Blackmon.

Shortly after this ad there were "shoe-jackings" in many American cities where people were robbed of their Air Jordan trainers. This level of popularity and impact on people embracing his prowess heralded a new position that a sportsperson holds in the psyche of the global community. His appearance on a brand immediately generated more sales for that company. This was the command he created for himself by his basketball mastery.

As another very famous name in basketball, Magic Johnson, has said: "There's Michael Jordan, and then the rest of us."

Jordan's achievements;
2 Olympic gold medals, 1984 & 1992
6 times NBA Champion
6 times NBA Most Valuable Player in Finals
5 times NBA MVP
10 times NBA scoring leader (1987–1993, 1996–1998)
14 NBA All-Star selections
3 times NBA All-Star Game MVP

The SALIENT QUALITIES OF 9 Fire CWF

MAKING THINGS VISUAL People wanted to see Jordan play.

PUSH IT TO THE LIMITS Jordan kept pushing himself.

REMOVING BOUNDARIES Jordan changed the way basketball is played with his "air suspension moves."

DEEP INNER EXPLORATION Jordan had peak performances under very adverse conditions suffering from flu in a NBA playoff game: he dominated the game. In his early NBA career in 1984, he created a lot of jealousy especially when playing against certain senior players where they did a "freeze out" of not passing him the ball. He was unaffected by this and still overpowered games. This requires deep mental resources.

TRAILBLAZER OF EPIC PROPORTIONS Jordan dominated NBA basketball and created a new approach to basketball.

DOMINANT LEADER IN THEIR CHOSEN FIELD This is totally evident.

ARE STRONGLY PASSIONATE ABOUT THEIR VIEWPOINTS & EXPRESSIONS Jordan played with total passion.

ARE CONSUMED BY WHAT THEY DO On the court Jordan was alight.

CONSCIOUS MASTER OF HER CONTEXTUAL WINNING FIELD

MARINA ABRAMOVIC

The function of the artist in a disturbed society
is to give awareness of the universe,
to ask the right questions,
and to elevate the mind.

Marina Abramovic

Marina Abramovic was born November 30th 1946 in Belgrade, in what was then Yugoslavia and is now Serbia. I only began exploring her work in early May 2014, although I had noted her name and birthdate as someone to research a number of months earlier. Then, as I was putting the finishing touches to the book, I looked at what she does and "where she speaks from".

This blew me away, and totally inspired me at the same time. What crowned it for me was a YouTube clip where she was explaining to this presenter "How to Drink Water". This is something that I had already been sharing with students and clients over the previous 6 months, and here she was talking the same language. In addition, her Contextual Winning Field is the 1 Water pattern.

Marina's approach to art from what I have observed is about pushing the limits of mind and body. In a way one can say she is constantly pushing the limits of the "states of water". She pushes herself, and I have to acknowledge here that some of the words I am using, to describe what I hear her really saying in an interview, are very limited. This may be because words cannot always fully capture what is being made available in her art.

Because of this, I will use her own quotes to best describe and acknowledge how she is manifesting her 1 Water Contextual Winning Field. I have chosen not to view what she is doing as an **Unconscious** doyenne of this field. She may not have articulated it in the exact same way that I have written it, but all her actions and expressions tell me she is conscious of this Field.

"Once you enter into the performance state you can push your body to do things you absolutely could never normally do."

"We always project into the future or reflect in the past, but we are so little in the present."

"Because of technology, we don't develop telepathy. We don't use telepathy, but use, you know, the mobile phones. Why?"

"To control the breathing is to control the mind. With different patterns of breathing, you can fall in love, you can hate someone, you can feel the whole spectrum of feelings just by changing your breathing."

She continually test her endurance levels with her performances: this is a core part of how she approaches her work as an artist.

An interesting aspect of her career were her joint performances with Ulay, a German performance artist who she met in 1976 in Amsterdam. They performed together for 12 years till 1988. Their collaboration had themes of ego, duality, oneness, loss of self and from what she has shared, all of this was experientially fulfilled. Ulay's birthday is November 30th 1943, giving him the pattern of 3 Wood as an Adult and 8 Earth as his Child Star number which surprise, surprise has him with a 1 Water Contextual Winning Field pattern as well.

Amazingly, in an interview he gave in 2011, he said that he has chosen whenever he meets someone to always introduce himself as Water. It does seem that these two individuals are very conscious of their Contextual Winning Fields.

Marina is now engaged with her own Institute in America called MAI (Marina Abramovic Institute). Visitors to the Institute undergo mind and body cleansing exercises devised by her. She teaches people her method for doing long durational performance pieces. When you take a succinct look at Marina Abramovic's creative expression as an artist you see all these qualities being very consciously expressed

1. She **OPERATES WITH CONFIDENCE IN THE INTANGIBLE DIMENSION OF LIFE**. In fact, she talks about this anytime she is given the opportunity to convey what her art is about.
2. She is **AN IMAGINATIVE CREATOR**, this is a given. No words are needed to expand on this.
3. She is **A SKILLFUL MASS COMMUNICATOR**: watch and listen to her in any clip on Youtube about her work, and she immediately enrolls you as she touches some aspect of us human beings that says this woman is totally authentic and walks her talk.
4. She is **A PERSEVERING VISIONARY**. She has been on this wavelength of pushing things beyond the limit with her art through her "stretching" of her mind and body for many decades.
5. She **ENJOYS SEEMINGLY EFFORTLESS ARTISTIC EXPRESSION**. The word "enjoy" may not be appropriate at all times with what she does, but seemingly effortless is surely present.

Marina Abramovic, The One Water Contextual Winning Field salutes you!

CHAPTER 7

Contextual winning case histories (when it worked and when it didn't)

You'll learn, as you get older,

that rules are made to be broken.

Be bold enough to live life on your terms,

and never, ever apologize for it.

Go against the grain, refuse to conform,

take the road less traveled

instead of the well-beaten path.

Laugh in the face of adversity,

and leap before you look.

Dance as though EVERYBODY is watching.

March to the beat of your own drummer.

And stubbornly refuse to fit in.

Mandy Hale

The Single Woman: Life, Love, and a Dash of Sass

CHAPTER 7
Contextual winning case histories
(when it worked and when it didn't)

GOING AGAINST THE GRAIN

John was born July 8 1963, which makes him a 1 Water personality as an adult and 3 Wood personality as a child. His CWF is the 2 Earth.

End of August 2002 he travelled by ferry from Holyhead in Wales to Dublin in Ireland, a North Westerly direction. Late August 2002 was a 2 Earth month in a 7 Metal star year. Travelling North West was heading into the 3 Wood star energy, which is the direction of his childhood star number. He was also moving in the direction opposite to his adult star number. (See chapter 13 of Grasshopping Through Time for the use of 9 Star Ki to determine auspicious directions of travel). Besides which, he was going on a journey where he was planning to sleep in his car on the coastline as he attended a program. This was all happening in his 2 Earth CWF month. Energetically this is very challenging at a time when it is best for him to keep risk to a minimum and use the energy of his 2 Earth CWF more creatively. To cut a long story short, he had a dose of radiation hit him from a discharge from a British Nuclear plant, which is on the west coast of England. The poison in his system left him sick for months, leaving him bed ridden. It took him more than a year to regain his energy and even then he had to be extremely cautious with his lifestyle and dietary habits.

FIASCO OF A HOUSE PURCHASE IN DOYO TIME FOR AN 8 EARTH CWF PERSONALITY

Doyo is an Oriental word for the "season" that occurs 9 days before and 9 days after the solstices and equinoxes; this time occurs four times a year and is a time of the Earth element.

Rita planned to make a house purchase in Las Vegas whilst living in Carlsbad in California. Rita was born June 25 1949, a 6 Metal star personality as an adult and a 1 Water personality as a child. Her CWF is the 8 Earth. Late August 1996, a 2 Earth month in a 4 Wood year, Rita flew to England on a business trip. She was heading East into the 9 Fire star energy. This is very difficult for a 6 metal star personality. Plus her priority was acquiring the new home. New homes are not like shoes, we do not buy them every month or year. The original plan was that when she returned from her business trip September 20, the new house would be purchased and waiting for her. Well, as the trip went on in Europe things were not happening for her home purchase. In fact it was turning into a disaster. Mortgage agreements that were all lined up were not happening. Accountants were making exorbitant requests for their services and adding new requirements for the deal to go through. Finally, on September 14 the house deal fell through and she had to return to America and drop her business trip to look for another home. She did eventually do this 72 hours later but with an exhausting effect on her energy. She was totally wiped out for 2 weeks, putting herself through one of the most stressful experiences in her life. Again, we return to the need for people who have Earth CWFs to honour the need for stabilising and focusing the energy plus slow is definitely fast for these individuals in the Doyo period.

SPINNING OUT OF CONTROL, DOING TOO MUCH. ACTIVATING DANGER SIGNS FOR THE 8 EARTH CWF PERSONALITY

Anne was born June 26 1958, she ran her own business from home. Anne is 6 Metal personality as an adult and a 1 Water as a child. Her CWF is the 8 Earth. There are times, many times when Anne has too many rods in the fire and this was one of them.

It was May 18 2001, an 8 Earth Star month in an 8 Earth star year. Rushing became the norm for more than 3 weeks. Her sleep was not restful. She would wake early with her mind racing. Then she broke a bottle in her bathroom area and in her panic in sorting it out stepped on the bottle and cut the sole of her left foot. This did not stop her, yes she had stitches put into her foot and was back racing. That month she made some disastrous business decisions that cost her thousands of pounds. On reflection, and with her awareness of the Grasshopping system, she has started to pay more attention to these tell-tale signs of honouring her 8 Earth CWF energy, especially during times when it is activated.

PUSHING BOUNDARIES IN DOYO TIME FOR 2 EARTH CWF PERSONALITY

Karin was born April 19 1957, she is a 7 Metal as an adult and a 6 Metal as a child. Her CWF is the 2 Earth star. Karin worked in the field of counselling and was excellent at her job, creating great rapport with her clients and expressing her care with insightful compassion. On September 23 2004, a 4 Wood star month in a 5 Earth Star year, she was invited to participate in a psychic healing circle with some business associates and colleagues. Karin spun out of control, experiencing disturbed sleep, nausea and a spaced out feeling for the next 3 days. This was outside of Karin's boundaries plus she was having some physical therapy for some of her own health challenges that week. It took her 3-4 weeks to come back to herself. The Doyo time was not a wise time for Karin to be exploring such dimensions in her life, not for her as a 2 Earth CWF personality.

MAKING CHANGES AND DOING ROUTINE THINGS WITH DISASTROUS EFFECTS IN DOYO TIME FOR 5 EARTH CWF PERSONALITY

Keith was born June 2 1971. He is a 2 Earth as an adult and an 8 Earth as a child. His CWF is the 5 Earth Star. On June 15 2004 he was repairing his car. Keith had postponed having his car serviced for some months. He was now in the doyo time, getting the full service done to his car, he wanted the "full works" done, so much so that he borrowed his brother's vehicle so the garage could have it for a day. That day he was reversing his brother's car and smashed up the rear end, creating havoc in his life for some weeks plus major expenses.

LETTING HEALTH ISSUES BUILD UP AND SUDDENLY BURSTING FORTH IN DOYO TIME FOR 2 EARTH CWF PERSONALITY

Hazel was born January 10 1940. She is a 7 Metal as an adult and a 6 Metal as a child. Her CWF is the 2 Earth star. Hazel is pretty conscientious about her health. She spends quite a sum on her herbs and food supplements. From time to time she lets it slip and comes off her program. This was such a time, her body had not been having any of her special restorative herbs for almost 2 months. She had also moved into a very active social life at the beginning of September.

September 14 2002, a doyo period, it happened, a clot occurred in her left leg that left her in agony to the extent that an ambulance was called and she was rushed to the emergency room in the hospital. Hazel is still recovering from this clot, some 5 years later.

NEW VIGOROUS EXERCISE PROGRAM RUNS INTO DISASTER IN DOYO TIME FOR 2 EARTH CWF PERSONALITY

Roy was born March 8 1946. He is a 9 Fire as an adult and a 4 Wood as a child. His CWF is the 2 Earth. Keeping fit is a major concern for Roy. He likes to view himself as being in his prime and in control of his body. That being said though he does have a major addiction to sweet items. This led to him having an overweight condition. This had got to him and he decided to embark on a major keep fit program beginning March 13 2001. The first day of the March Doyo period was when he embarked on this intensive keep-fit program. He enjoyed cycling along the lanes in the country side and so he decided he would cycle an hour very vigorously every day to burn his fat off. That first day after 20 minutes he ran into a huge stone in the road and off he came, hitting the ground with a major thud breaking 2 ribs and leaving him incapacitated for 6 weeks with no intense keep fit program. He felt very disappointed.

SIR DONALD CAMPBELL AND HIS ENDEAVOURS

Sir Donald Campbell was born 23.3.1921, making him a double 7 Metal Star personality with 9 Fire as his Wisdom Star.

He was the son of Sir Malcolm Campbell, holder of 13 world speed records in the 1920s and 1930s in the famous Bluebird cars and boats. Campbell began his speed record attempts using his father's old boat Bluebird K4, but after a structural failure at 170 mph (270 km/h) on Coniston Water, Lancashire in 1951 he developed a new boat.

Designed by Ken and Lew Norris, the Bluebird K7 was an all-metal jet-propelled 3-point hydroplane with a Metropolitan-Vickers Beryl jet engine producing 3,500 lb/ft (16 kN) of thrust.

Campbell set seven world water speed records in K7 between 1955 and 1964. The first was at Ullswater on 23 July 1955, where he set a record of 202.15 mph (324 km/h). The series of speed increases-216 mph (348 km/h) later in 1955, 225 mph (362 km/h) in 1956, 239 mph (385 km/h) in 1957, 248 mph (399 km/h) in 1958, 260 mph (420 km/h) in 1959-peaked on 31 December 1964 at Dumbleyung Lake, Western Australia when he reached 276.33 mph (444.71 km/h); he remains the world's most prolific breaker of water speed records.

On 4 January 1967, Campbell was killed when Bluebird K7 flipped and disintegrated at a speed in excess of 300 mph (480 km/h) on Conniston Water, in The Lake District.

Bluebird had completed a perfect North-South run at an average of 297.6 mph (478.9 km/h), and Campbell used a new water brake to slow K7 from her peak speed of 315 mph (507 km/h). Instead of refueling and waiting for the wash of this run to subside, as had been pre-arranged, Campbell decided to make the return run immediately.

The second run was even faster; as K7 passed the start of the measured kilometre, it was travelling at over 320 mph (510 km/h). However, the craft's stability had begun to break down as it travelled over the rough water, and the boat started tramping from sponson to sponson. 150 yards (140 m) from the end of the measured mile, Bluebird lifted from the surface and took off at a 45-degree angle. It somersaulted and plunged back into the lake, nose first.

The boat then cartwheeled across the water before coming to rest. The impact broke Bluebird forward of the air intakes and the main hull sank shortly afterwards. Campbell had been killed instantly.

4 January 1967 was a 7 Metal Star month in a 7 Metal star year. This would be a most inappropriate time to make such an attempt. Yes, he succeeded and he paid the price with his life. Two aspects were going against the energy for this attempt.

Firstly, it was winter in Britain, the time of Water challenging the 9 Fire Star that was Campbell's Wisdom Star. Energetically, winter is a time of rest and quiet: Campbell was going for the biggest exertion of adrenalin.

 The second aspect that was going against him was the 7 Metal Star month in a 7 Metal Star year. This would be time to stabilize things, a time to be very practical and minimize risks.

When he broke the record on Dec 31 1964, at Lake Dumbleyung in Perth, Western Australia it was summer, the Fire energy season. 1964 was a 9 Fire year, the year of his Wisdom Star, while December 1964 was a 4 Wood Star month.

In that month (December 1964, when he set the world record), Campbell's 7 Metal Stars were in the 8 Earth house.

For the 9 Fire year (1964 was a 9 Fire year), the 8 Earth house is occupied by the 3 Wood Star. The 3 Wood star here gives spontaneity, competitiveness and explosive energy. His choice of timing was deeply insightful and his efforts were justly rewarded.

Interestingly, although the colour blue has no specific effect on the 9 Fire Wisdom Star personality, the red felt jacket of Campbell's lucky mascot, Mr Whoppit, matches the colour of his Wisdom Star. Campbell refused to race unless Mr. Whoppit was with him in the cockpit.

CORE CONTEXTUAL WINNING FIELD APPROACHES
9 FIRE

1. BE DOMINANT LEADER IN YOUR CHOSEN FIELD
2. ENJOY WORKING UP A SWEAT
3. BE STRONGLY PASSIONATE ABOUT YOUR VIEWPOINTS AND EXPRESSIONS
4. BE CONSUMED BY WHAT YOU DO
5. BE A PIONEER
6. ENJOY MAKING THINGS VISUAL

PABLO PICASSO AND "GUERNICA", THE PAINTING OF THE 20TH CENTURY

On May 1, 1937, four days after the bombing of Guernika shocked the world, Picasso, gripped by urgency and rage, made his first preparatory drawing. Over the next month, he made some 30 drawings for the painting, and of course, the masterpiece Guernica itself.

Picasso was born 25 October 1881, making him a 2 Earth personality as an adult and a 3 Wood personality as a child. His CWF is the 7 Metal Star. This Contextual Winning Field is about aesthetics, beauty, harmony, and the harvest, the reaper of the harvest. 1937 was a 9 Fire year. His 2 Earth star was in the 7 Metal house for this year. 7 Metal house is the house of the harvest, the reaping of things.

The beginning of May 1937 was a 3 Wood month. 3 Wood is Picasso's child star number. In this position his childhood issues can easily arise, plus issues that carry strong emotional responses with great feelings of vulnerability and helplessness. As a child, his emotional response would have been rage and here with this incident happening before his very eyes rage is what bit into his heart. In Picasso's creative process with this painting we have his emotional nature being triggered. This triggering is extended throughout the month of May when he works on this painting with over 50 outlines being done on it.

From 6 May 1937, the 2 Earth star is being activated as we move into a 2 Earth month. This puts Picasso into the core of his disturbing emotion Grief, which would have been palpable in Guernica in that month. His painting was first displayed at the Spanish Pavilion at the Paris World's Fair in late July 1937. This was a double 9 fire period. July 1937 is a 9 fire month in a 9 fire year. Here again we return to the aspect of the reaping of the harvest in Picasso's life. This is a grim harvest and fully expresses the core grief that was such a part of Picasso's life. This rough core and relentless drive to dominate in his relationships with women was a masking of the grief that was there for him constantly. Picasso has made that frustration of being grief- stricken, filled with rage yet unable to make any palpable difference, which is the truth for the vast majority of human beings on the planet. The evidence of this truth was made very clear a short while after.

What followed 2 years after this painting was created was the start of the Second World War, the genocide against the Jews, the deaths of more than 10 million human beings during this period. This carnage has continued and is a signature of the last 70 years of the expression called human beings.

Where Picasso used his 7 Metal CWF qualities was to craft a painting that was proportioned and harmonic with all its painful and gut- wrenching images. He was also able to capture a kinesthetic quality with Guernica, something happens to your guts and skin when you look at this painting. The emotions move to your skin rather than remains in your eyes. Another aspect of the 7 Metal Contextual Winning Field that Picasso is connecting with is capturing and harvesting what is happening in that moment. This gruesome incident happened at a market in the late afternoon, whilst people were purchasing the harvest of the region. This theme, unfortunately, is the background harvest that is an inherent part of our modern lives. Wherever it has been displayed, Picasso's Guernica provokes controversy.

Here are some examples:

When it was first displayed at the World's Fair in Paris late July 1937

The main attraction, Picasso's Guernica, was anything but a celebration of the marvels of technology. Many found it repulsive and contrary to the spirit of the Exhibition - even those who were sympathetic to the cause. "If you can't in a political painting very clearly point out the good guys and the bad guys," explains Art Historian Patricia Failing, "or very clearly identify the characters in symbolic terms, this is something that's difficult for people who have expectations based on earlier concepts of political paintings."

"I paint this way because it's a result of my thought," Picasso responded. "I have worked for years to obtain this result: I can't use an ordinary manner just to have the satisfaction of being understood!"

One notable exception to the bad press was the prestigious French journal, Cahiers d'Art. Featuring Guernica in a double issue, Picasso's creation is defended and celebrated with emotional tributes and eloquent writings from many intellectuals and artists: "These visionary forms have an evocative power greater than shapes drawn with every realistic detail. They challenge people to truly comprehend the effects of their actions." (Christian Zervos)

"Our epoch is grand, dramatic and dangerous, and Picasso, because he is equal to his circumstances, makes a picture worthy of them." Guernica is an "appalling drama of a great people abandoned to the tyrants of the Dark Ages . . .All the world can see, can understand, this immense Spanish tragedy." (Amedé Ozenfant)

The stark, disturbing vision, once dismissed as "the dream of a madman," proved prophetic when Europe was plunged into a war that engulfed the world.

United Nations Security Council in New York February 2003

The United Nations in New York has a copy of Guernica in tapestry, donated by Nelson Rockefeller (who had to accept this as second best when Picasso refused to sell him the original). It hangs in a corridor outside the Security Council's meeting room, where it acts as a visible conscience.

In 2003, however, when Colin Powell attempted to scare the UN into legitimizing the Iraq war, the tapestry was suddenly covered by a blue shroud. A spokesman explained that its blacks, whites and greys confused the television cameras; the truth, is that the tapestry derided the American officials who so sanctimoniously briefed the press while standing in front of it. This censorship recognizes the contemporaneity of Guernica. The mouths of its figures, like wounds, still gape open and the silent screams they emit are audible to everyone except the militarists they accuse.

JAMES DEAN ACCIDENT

James Dean was born 08.02.1931, he was a 6 Metal star person as an adult and a 8 Earth as a child. (See chapter 3 in "Grasshopping Through Time" for explanation of why 5 Earth changes to 8 Earth.) On 30 September 1955 he died in a car accident the day before finishing the movie "Giant". Here we have the accident happening in a 7 metal star month in a 9 Fire star year. 7 Metal was James Dean's CWF, he had just finished the movie "Giant", substantial parts of which were filmed during his 7 Metal CWF month. From 1956 when "Giant" was released till 1970 it was Warner Bros highest grossing film. Much of that was due to the fascination that people had with James Dean as an individual and his skills as an actor. He was spoken of in the same breath at the time as Marlon Brando. His personality was that magnetic and his character that present and independent, he was the other rebel in Hollywood, Brando being the other one. To go from a movie set, which he had been on since July 1955 and switch gears to head to a car-racing meet in a Doyo time in his CWF month was pushing against the energetic grain in a big way. Here is an excerpt of what the BBC reported about the incident. I quote:

"The wheel of his German-made Porsche sports car when it was involved in a head-on collision with another car 30 miles (48 km) east of Paso Robles this evening. Mr. Dean's mechanic, Rolph Wutherich, who was a passenger in the car, was taken to hospital with serious injuries.

Medics said Mr. Dean, who was dead on arrival at hospital, suffered a broken neck and numerous broken bones. At the time of the accident the road racing enthusiast was on his way to a race meeting at Salinas, California."

The Double 7 Metal Star Personality
The Singer: The Red Dress, their 9 CWF Colour.

The Red Dress

"The V-necked red dress was perfect. Not that jarring-bright orangey red, but a softer red with pink undertones. I'd tried on "red-everythings" for days; red skirts, tank tops, blouses, even sandals. Everything but red socks. I was seeing red everywhere; drawn to a red book cover with total disregard for its contents, a red box of chocolates, and red table clothes.

Rex told me I should wear red. At the time I had three basic wardrobe colours. When I packed for long trips, I used a colour coding system for arranging the clothes in my well-worn suitcase. The sophisticated grey and black attire for city wear was folded neatly next to the khaki and army green safari clothes for my excursions to Africa. For trips to warmer climes everything was in shades of blue, which my mother assured me went well with my blue eyes and blond hair. "Very soft. Feminine." Not bold, not "in your face". Not red.

It was time for a little audacity. I'd been fighting depression for a few months. "Red" seemed to hold out the possibility of parties, and sudden dynamic change. If Rex said so then maybe it could push me out of my funk. It was certainly an experiment worth trying.

I inaugurated my red dress at a conference ... where I witnessed for the first time the red-phenomena. I was definitely more outgoing when I wore red. I felt vibrant, literally, as if the cells of my body were buzzing at a higher energetic level. I spoke with greater confidence and ease. People seemed to notice me more, and frankly I loved the attention. I rose to the occasion. Even my posture changed. I held myself differently. I made myself taller. You can't slouch when you're in red.

You can't hide from the world either. It seeks you out…or so it seemed. I was surprised to find I'd been given a full scholarship to a three year course by someone I'd just met…on the day I was wearing that dress. Was I presenting a more dynamic picture of myself to the world when I was in red? And was that drawing a different type of person and new opportunities to me?

This past April I was in the town of Oaxaca, Mexico, a World Heritage Site where buildings pose next to each other in colourful juxtaposition. Taxis are pink…or blue, or aqua marine or yellow or a faded wine-colored red. The traditional costumes of the numerous indigenous groups vary widely in their design but not in their choice of colours, all embroidered in the brightest shades. During the Semana Santa, on Good Friday, the statues of Jesus and Mary were paraded through the streets by men in full length satin gowns and hoods of bright purple.

Just after my return to New York, with Mexico's joyful colours still exploding in my head, I left the house in the sleeveless red dress on an exceptionally warm spring day. But on the train into Manhattan, with a mounting sense of discomfort, I discovered what a horribly "gauche" fashion mistake I'd made. I did a colour check, looking up and down the aisles of the car: black, navy, brown, grey, khaki and white. One yellow tie.

I stood in the main hall at Grand Central station under its famous clock and watched people come and go. In spite of the shift in the weather there was a wintry mood in the air. More of the same dark, dull shades. A brief a glimpse of a red blouse stifled by a navy suit jacket. I hit the streets. Concrete grey and black tar… my gaze climbed the buildings, searching out the brilliant sun soaked sky.

But I wasn't the only one longing for colour against the drab background of the city that day. When I walked into my breakfast meeting one woman actually cried out "What a fabulous dress!" That was all I needed to get me back up and running. That morning I was recording my first Voice Over session as a result of a casting call from a brand new agent, so I was anxious to make a good impression. Part of that entailed establishing a good relationship with the producer and putting everyone at ease. That's why I'd worn the dress… to incite the now familiar confidence I felt in red. I broke the ice with stories of Mexico... the colour, the dancing, the light. As a result, we exchanged anecdotes and conversation flowed easily. Even though the script turned out to be a pretty tough "read"... trying to make legal "speak" sound conversational... we waded through it gracefully. And of course they wanted me back.

Rex's red dress is in the wash again. My wardrobe grows to accommodate more of the same. I've vowed to wear red to every single audition in the future... even though I only do off-camera work. It's the feel of red that works for me. The me who steps up to the challenge. The me who stands out in a crowd. The me who makes bold statements about life and beauty and love and music and never, never apologises for who she is.

My father was a B chord and my mother was a C.
Coming down through a counterpoint to a closer
harmony.
The result was a baby song feeling for a melody.
The rhythm bounce when it touch the ground that's
how I came to be 1.2, 1.2, 1, 2, 3, 4.
Hold the tempo for me.
Jump in the line in front and behind and march to the
1, 2, 3, all roads lead to the cemetery.

Andre Tanker

The Last Bit

Man is a microcosm, or a little world,

because he is an extract from all the stars and

planets of the whole firmament,

from the earth and the elements;

and so he is their quintessence.

Paracelsus

Time and its subtle influence on our lives have been laid out for you in this book. You have seen how birthdate, linked with the 9 Star Ki Calendar, gives you your Adult an Child Star Numbers PLUS Your Contextual Winning Field.

You have become conscious of your Time DNA, the Matrix which allows you to engage with life from a new place.

You have discovered a new companion, your Contextual Winning Field.

Cultivating your relationship with your Contextual Winning Field will open new possibilities in how you live your life.

In your hands is a guidebook that will move you away from the "24/7 Monster" view of time to a new relationship, where Time becomes your friend.

Now you know your Contextual Winning Field, you can go to Chapter 3 and follow the guidance given there: embrace the qualities that are highlighted for your CWF pattern and let them become as instinctive as your breathing. As this unfolds, observe what new insights start showing up in your life.

These observations would reinforce your partnership with your Time DNA, your Contextual Winning Field.

Give yourself permission to celebrate this daily by manifesting more creative ways of living your life. Your Contextual Winning Field will always serve you and is a core relationship in your life.

I will continue to add more data to my website www.thetimeofyourlifebook.com Please do check it out on a regular basis, as this is my ongoing support for you as you embrace your Contextual Winning Field. It is a joyful celebration of life's beauty, harmony and elegance.

Enjoy,
Rex Lassalle

We do not know it because we are fooling away our time with outward and perishing things, and are asleep in regards to that which is real within ourself.

Paracelsus

Appendix

Essential Oils contain minerals.

Essential Oils are a catalyst because

they are made up of oxygen, amino acids

and their function is to carry nutrients

into the cells of the human body..

D. Gary Young

Founder of Young Living Essential Oils

APPENDIX

SOLUTIONS

In this book I have presented many approaches for connecting with your Contextual Winning Field. Yet, because of the pace of our modern life and the environments in which we live there are stresses and toxic levels that we need to manage and have resources that we can use that work.

Here are some suggestions for you to handle some common challenges that many of us face.

1. Electromagnetic pollution. I have outlined "What to do to neutralize it" There is a Ritual for this using Marma points.
   http://theocoteanewsletter.com/2012/10/

2. In the second section I explain "What to take to counteract it."
   http://theocoteanewsletter.com/2012/11/

SLEEP ISSUES

So many of us have challenges to get a good night's sleep. Here are some suggestions to change that experience that insomnia, nightmares and restless nights become something that happened in the past.
http://theocoteanewsletter.com/?s=Your+special+moments

YOUR EYES

We spend hours in front of our computers every day plus texting and looking into small screens. Here are some eye exercises that can make a difference. Good to get the habit of spending a bit of time doing this everyday. It will create a big benefit to your energy levels and emotions.

Our eyes are experiencing higher levels of stress and pollution than they have ever experienced before. For most people in the modern world, their eyes are glued everyday to a computer screen or some handheld electronic device, straining to read small fonts and sending and receiving messages. Our eyes have no idea how best to respond to this intense demand on their capacity to provide information to our nervous systems.

Here are some exercises and techniques that can make a difference.

1. Start by massaging the Marma points on your eyebrows. See chart in Appendix. If you have Young Living Essential Oil's Frankincense, put a hint of it on both your middle fingers and work the top of your eyebrows, then do the same immediately under your eyebrows. Be very cautious that you do not get the oil into your eyes, hence the suggestion of it being a hint of oil. Give yourself permission to breathe gently, allowing a sense of spaciousness to fill your chest and rib cage as you work on these points.

2. Put a hint more of the Frankincense on your right middle finger and gently massage it into the tip of your nose. Spend some time doing this, about two minutes: this opens up the heart space and in so going gives the liver, which governs the eyes, an opportunity to relax and nourish the eyes with its energy.

3. Move to the Marma point AKSHAKA, located on either side of your sternocleidomastoid muscles on the neck, just above the clavicle. Again, put a hint of Frankincense on your middle fingers and press them into these two points, while slowly turning your head to the left and right as you breathe gently and

allow your eyes to have a restful gaze as you turn your head to the left and right. Do this for a minute.

4. Rub the palm of your hands together to make them warm, and then slowly cover your closed eyes with your palms and do some gentle deep breathing for a minute.

5. Clasp your first fingers over your thumbnails, then gently rub the backs of your thumbs together till they are warm. Then make outward circles with the back of your thumbs around your eyes as you keep your forefingers above your eyebrows. Do 36 circles.

6. Finally, put two drops of Frankincense in the palms and rub your hands briskly till they feel very warm. Place your warm palms over your eyes, keeping them open, and allow the fine Frankincense molecules to stimulate your eyes. In a short while your eyes will begin streaming. Do hold them over your open eyes for as long as you can. Wipe your eyes with a tissue and not with your fingers. Rest for a minute then repeat 2 more times.

7. Doing this consistently on a daily basis can create major improvements with your vision. ENJOY.

FINDING EXTRA SUPPORT

Many of us experience exhaustion at times feeling overwhelmed with the many things we need to accomplish in our day. Somehow we all wish to find some extra support from somewhere. Look no further here are some tailored made suggestions that relate specifically to your personal Contextual Winning Field.

These are some Young Living Essential Oils that I have found over the last 4 years have created a big difference for my students and clients. There are 3 simple ways that you can use them.

1. Rub them under the soles of your feet, then cup your hands bring your hands to your nostrils and inhale the fragrance from the soles of your feet in a deep and relaxed manner for a minute or two.

2. Many have found putting a drop or two of the oil on their navel and massaging it into the skin brings a new glow of energy to them. Should you feel slightly uncomfortable in doing this you can put a bit of almond oil or coconut oil on your navel before massaging the oil into the navel.

3. Putting some drops in the palm of your hands or rubbing the Roll On that is linked to your Contextual Winning Field then spending a few minutes to breathe this deeply into your system. Does create a major boost to your energy field.

Should you fine that you have a strong reaction to the oils, this can indicate that your body is starting to detox by interacting with the molecules of the oils. This occasionally happens to some people who are exceedingly acidic. The molecules of the oils are that fine and subtle that they are starting to chelate the petrochemicals that are locked in our cells. Detoxing your system and consuming foods that are more alkaline in nature can easily rectify this.

WHAT ARE THE OILS FOR THE DIFFERENT CONTEXTUAL WINNING FIELDS?

Here are the oils that I have seen work best with supporting the different Contextual Winning Fields.

1 CWF	VALOR/ BALSAM FIR
2 CWF	EXODUS II
3 CWF	JUVA CLEANSE
4 CWF	GERMAN CHAMMOMILE
5 CWF	OCOTEA
6 CWF	DEEP RELIEF ROLL ON
7 CWF	BREATHE AGAIN ROLL ON

8 CWF   DI GIZE

9 CWF C   YPRESS

HOW TO GET THE OILS

This is how you would set up your account with Young Living to order the items you want, so to become a member:

- go to www.youngliving.com, select your country, this will take you to the homepage of Young Living
- go to top right corner of this homepage - member signup/virtual office login
- select member signup - become a member - fill in your selection asa wholesale member. Of course you can fill in as a retail customer but then you pay 24% more for the products.
- in the sponsor field put the number 1155053 , In the enroller field please put 1117477
- continue to fill in your details - make note of the password and PIN details and your ensuing member ID number issued next to your username. You will need these details when you go into your virtual office to do any online orders, or when communicating on anything to do with Young Living.